The
Silva Solution

The
Silva Solution

BUILDING BLACK BELTS FROM THE INSIDE OUT

Greg **Silva**

Library of Congress Cataloging-in-Publication Data

To Lester

To be honest, I don't remember Lester's last name. At age 13, he and I had words at a pick up baseball game that ended with me on the ground with a black eye and broken nose. The next day, my father enrolled me in martial arts, and I never stopped. That single punch not only changed my nose, but my life and the life of thousands of students in many different countries.

CONTENTS

FOREWORD ix

ACKNOWLEDGEMENTS xiii

INTRODUCTION xvii

CHAPTER ONE: Broken Kids 1

CHAPTER TWO: It's Not What You Teach,
It's How You Teach It
That's Important 7

CHAPTER THREE: Classroom Mechanics:
It's Not About You –
It's All About Them.............. 15

CHAPTER FOUR: The After-Class Checklist....25

CHAPTER FIVE: The Benefit Driven School...33

CHAPTER SIX: Winning Over Parents.......... 43

CHAPTER SEVEN: Curriculum Integration.........55

CHAPTER EIGHT: It's Becoming Clear.............. 63

CHAPTER NINE: Become Remarkable 73

CHAPTER TEN: Keeping Your Black Belts
Your Black Belts.................... 83

CHAPTER ELEVEN: The Last Chapter of
This Book – However,
The Story is Not Over... 97

FOREWORD

THERE HAVE ONLY BEEN two times in my entire life that I have felt totally over my head. Once was when I stepped into the ring to fight the legendary Billy Blanks. The other was when my mentor and friend, Greg Silva, asked me to write this forward. How do you choose the words that will capture and express not only how I feel about this man, but the impact he has had on my life, and, literally hundreds of thousands of others? I pray the following will give you a glimpse into the man whom I have had the privilege of working with for over sixteen years.

I first met Mr. Silva when I was only sixteen years old. I used to regularly attend and compete at his local karate tournament. Later, at the age of nineteen, Mr. Silva became my mentor. I was operating a little martial arts school in Rhode Island and I began to hear of what seemed like impossible success.

Back when it was considered to be a success if you ran a school of 300 students, Mr. Silva was running a school of over 1,200! Since then, life has been a perpetual nonstop learning process under his mentoring.

Throughout the sixteen years of our friendship, I could easily write my own book with all the lessons I've learned from him. Not just lesson about business, but lessons about life. Through his example, I've learned how to market a business, but also how to have fun while running my business. He's taught me that our business should be a blessing to your customers, but should also improve the quality of your life as well. I've learned how to laugh more, keep things simple, and how to develop the potential of others by investing in them.

I guess what makes Master Silva a genius in my book is his continual thinking "outside the box," and his uncanny ability to motivate others to higher and higher levels of success.

His ability to think outside the box was clearly seen at his school in Coral Springs, Florida. He was the first person to design a curriculum that was age specific. Most schools were still trying to teach adult material to kids. His was one of the first schools to put painted graphics on the walls, use music in class, and offer different colored and styles of uniforms for his students. He also created the first rotating curriculum which revolutionized the martial arts industry. He had the first school to offer events that made the school a social environment, not just an educational facility. To this day, thousands of schools are either just learning, or are teaching methods that he created 20 years ago. His teaching concepts and marketing style no doubt revolutionized our schools and catapulted our industry into the mainstream.

However, I think by far, one of the greatest attributes that I love about Mr. Silva is his desire to share his success and bring others to higher levels.

He enjoys life to the fullest and wants to see you enjoy life as well. His sense of possibility is contagious, and you want to be more successful just being around him. I have seen him over the years coach, direct, and guide many of our industries top icons. He's taking young, energetic students like myself with meager success and catapulted their careers to levels they never imagined. I've seen him take instructors whose careers were spiraling downward and out of control and taught them to become C.E.O. of million dollar organizations. I've seen him help those whose future looked dismal and teach them to run businesses that thrive. Without a doubt, our industry is not only different, but better, because of his impact.

As much as I know him as a business mentor, I know him even better as a friend. I have seen a side to Mr. Silva that few have ever seen. Not because he's hard to get close to, but because few people have ever tried. Most have only wanted to know him as the business guru, but I have gotten to know his heart. Seeing how much he loves and cares about people is evident at any Black Belt Graduation – as he wells up in tears watching men, woman, and children of any age realize their dream of becoming black belts for the first time. It's clear to see that he enjoys seeing people experience joy, success and the realization that they can achieve their dreams.

In closing, I would like to personally thank Mr. Silva for the many things he's taught me over the years. You've given me confidence in myself by giving me the opportunity to realize my potential. Your encouragement and inspirational words have always given me comfort whenever I needed it. Because of you, I have not only experienced a level of success I would no doubt never have realized alone, but myself and my family have lived a much more fulfilling and rewarding life because of your example. Thank you!

– *Paul Garcia*

Acknowledgements

WHEN I WAS EIGHTEEN, I was teaching martial arts part-time, I thought I was ready to open my own school and make my mark in the martial arts industry. Thankfully, I had parents who knew better and insisted I attend college and complete my education. After four years of business and psychology training, I was a little better prepared. Although there are countless people to thank, I must say my parents had the most influence on my life and success.

The support I have received from my children, family, students, team members and friends were all building blocks in the evolution of a unique teaching style. In the end, though, it was Ed Parker and his wisdom, analogies, jokes and his ability to communicate and educate I give thanks to. I had a unique opportunity to spend quite a bit of time with him as a student and a friend.

I also would like to acknowledge my editor, Herb Borkland, who motivated me, coaxed me and pushed me over 24 months to finish this book. His encouragement and patience is amazing.

My instructor, Ed Parker, the founder of American Kenpo, used to ask, "Why do Kenpo instructors have rounded shoulders and flat foreheads? It's because I will ask you a question and you shrug you shoulders. I then tell you the answer, which is so obvious you slap yourself in the head!"

INTRODUCTION

THIS ONE INTRODUCTORY call in particular started off like hundreds of others I've handled over the years. I had a mom on the other end of the line looking for information about martial arts lessons for her son.

An appointment was made for the next day, and I confirmed the information, gave her directions and was about to say, "Thank you," when the women said, "I do have to warn you that my son has a 'H – A – I – R' problem."

Okay, well, the response for this wasn't in my script manual, so I just replied, "Okay. I will see you and Carl tomorrow. Thanks for calling."

Next day, it's about time for Carl's first lesson, and I am getting everything ready for greeting my new student. It's a cold day in Connecticut, and Carl and his mom enter the school all bundled up to keep warm.

I quickly introduce myself to the family. Carl is seven years old and a little shy – nothing out of the ordinary, since most kids enrolling in our school have come because their parents are looking for some kind of life skill change.

I presented Carl with his uniform and asked him to remove his shoes, coat and hat before I showed him to the dressing room. It was then I found out

Carl's "H – A – I – R" problem. The boy was completely bald.

His mom just smiled at me, and I smiled at Carl, and we proceeded as if everything were normal. I later learned he suffered from a rare disease that resulted in loss of hair.

On the way to change clothes, we passed a banner in the school that read, "THIS IS A BLACK BELT SCHOOL". When I hung that banner, I took it very seriously. To me it meant that if I did my job correctly, anyone walking into my school should be able to make it to black belt.

I thought to myself, "Carl here is going to need the 'bonsai' treatment". Because I knew, to build *this* black belt, I would have to do it from the inside out. Just like Mr. Miagi.

"Wax on – wax off." Martial artist or not, I am sure you remember those lines from the movie "The Karate Kid". That one movie did more for the martial arts industry than any other event in history! Schools instantly became flooded with parents looking for lessons for their children. School owners figuring that martial arts builds self-esteem, confidence, courage, pride, patience and perseverance, began an advertising blitz; and the phrase "Karate Teaches Kids A Lot" was the theme.

But there turned out to be a major stumbling block. Up to this point, most martial arts schools were adult oriented. Martial artists refer to this era as "old school" – ninety minute classes, hard workouts, strict discipline.

Even so, *no problem*, many instructors felt. "Hey, I saw 'The Karate Kid'. Mr. Myagi had Daniel washing his car, wax his car; he painted the fence from morning to night and sanded floors for hours on end. If Daniel did it wrong, Mr. Myagi would just say, 'No, not that way. Do it *this* way'. So, it's no different teaching kids than adults, right? For Pete's sake, they *need* that! After all, it's hard work and strict discipline that create the confidence and self-esteem of a black belt".

Enrolling students, at this time, was easy. But, despite signing up more students, many schools were not experiencing any growth. Students did enroll, but then quit within a short amount of time.

Now, although owning a martial arts school is a business, what really drives most owners is not the money but the chance to make a difference to someone. In "The Karate Kid," the character Daniel started off as a good, quiet boy who was a victim of bullies. He had been pushed to the point where he just wanted to give up and have his mom move him away. Yet, after becoming a karate student, he was confident, centered and balanced.

So now the instructors began worrying. "Daniel didn't quit. Why do my students quit? If they just stayed with it long enough, I could make a big difference."

Daniel was "broken" when he started. What I mean by "broken" is that *there was something going on in his life he couldn't handle or change*. His mother was unable to help because she didn't understand. Then, as now, many of the thousands of kids enrolling in schools across the country were doing so because they, too, were also "broken."

Parents would find themselves at their wits' end, trying to deal with lack of control, no respect, no discipline or self-confidence, and so, in need of help, they were responding to those "Karate Teaches Kids A Lot" ads. Of course, they couldn't just come right out and say, "Hey, my kid's broken – fix him," but that was really what they were looking for.

My new student's mother had mentioned his "H – A – I – R" problem. What she was really trying to say is "My son has a challenge that has resulted in him being shy, afraid, not wanting to go to school. His education is suffering. I need some help. He's a great kid and doesn't deserve this."

In Chapter One, we will discuss how kids get broken and explore proven ways to reverse negative beliefs in a very short time through martial arts.

I mentioned earlier that, if I was going to transform Carl into a black belt, he needed the "bonsai" treatment – "to be built from the inside out". To make a difference in Carl's life, I had to be sure he wouldn't quit when things got a little tough or a little routine. I needed to work with him for the next thirty-six months if his black belt were to become a reality. After all, in the movie, Daniel didn't quit because he got the "bonsai" treatment. I just had to make sure I did the same for Carl.

Why "bonsai"? Remember how the movie went? Way before Daniel learned any actual karate, Mr. Myagi befriended and challenged the boy. One of the first things they did together was to work on little miniature bonsai trees. Mr. Myagi taught Daniel how to do the trimming, praised his abilities and kept on encouraging him. First, he built up trust in their relationship, then he was able to help Daniel believe in himself enough to accomplish a new challenge. He had developed in Daniel a sense of pride.

This, of course, is why Daniel didn't quit his karate lessons. What made the difference was a relationship of trust with his teacher and a growing belief in himself, both of which were created before the "real" karate was taught. Daniel-*san* is what I mean by a black belt created from the inside out, and how this can be done is what I call the "bonsai" treatment.

So the Silva Solution is about change. It's about thinking differently, looking at challenges from a new perspective and not being afraid to do what it takes to get the results your students deserve.

A good friend of mine, Paul Garcia and I began an Instructor Training program in 1994 to teach these principles to other instructors. The underlying theme was "It's not about you, it's all about them". In coming chapters, you will discover some bold moves I made, some radical thinking and reasoning that, by 1993, had brought 1,340 active students into my school, East West Karate.

The Silva Solution will start with one concept - to "Build Black Belts From the Inside Out," and then continue with the details, structure and creativity needed to make your students and your school a success. If you are not a school owner or instructor, the same tools can be applied to your family, work place, or personal life, but, basically, this is a Black Belt School's Black Belt Book. Meaning; as a school owner, your goal is to develop your students into black belts.

Over thirty-six months, you want those students to get in the best shape of their lives while learning the skills to defend themselves or their loved ones. And during this same period of time, you must also instill confidence, self-esteem, courage, patience, respect, courtesy, and indomitable spirit.

It's the goal of this book to give you some solutions so you can impact more people, make a positive difference and use your martial arts talents to literally change the world around you.

Now let's begin.

CHAPTER ONE

BROKEN KIDS

MY STUDENT CARL had developed a medical condition called *alopecia areata,* which caused his hair loss. Most likely something went wrong in his genetic make-up. However, the majority of parents seeking our help for childhood character issues – low self-esteem, a lack of confidence and courage, painful shyness, discourtesy, and disrespect – do not have kids born with these challenges. So, it is usually only after putting up with a lot of disturbing behavior, and having tried and failed by themselves, that the parents finally come to your school, asking for you to fix their "broken child".

What specialists call "limiting beliefs" cause these problems in children. It is extremely important we understand how a child forms limiting beliefs if we are going to be able to provide help. And, of course, we can be of help, we do so all the time in our schools, and so *our first step to building black belts from the inside out must be taken by changing these limiting beliefs to "empowering beliefs"*.

All beliefs, whether empowering or disempowering, are created by a series of what are called "references," or life experiences. The more references, the stronger the beliefs.

GREG SILVA

Tony Robbins uses the great illustration of a table, with the table top being your belief. The more legs the table has, the stronger it supports that belief. But, a table with less than four legs would be very weak and couldn't even support a single belief.

It was my father's belief that he was lucky and great at finding money. I use this illustration because it is fascinating to see how something, which to many people, would seem so far-fetched can actually become a very powerful conviction. My father took a walk every day, and on most days would come back with some coins. In fact, he saved all the coins he found during the year to take my mom to dinner on their annual vacation.

Now, people aren't born lucky, and money just doesn't fall in your path, but what I suspect is, early on, he did find some coins and so began believing he had this special gift, and this belief resulted in keeping him on the lookout for money as he went walking around. While most of us look straight ahead and all around us, my father kept expecting to find something valuable, so he looked down more often than most of us, resulting in him finding more than most of us.

By the way, this story is the basis of my own belief systems. The first is that beliefs are a result of constant references that support an idea. In other words, my father actually did keep finding money. And this also illustrates how, because of our beliefs, we tend to manifest in our lives what we truly expect will happen.

In Zig Ziglar's book *"Raising Positive Kids in a Negative World,"* he mentions that children are exposed to "eighty percent negative influence" throughout the day. So is it any wonder so many young people come to martial arts with a lack of self-confidence and poor self-esteem?

Kids are often cruel to each other. I really can't imagine any normal seven year old named Johnny getting on his school bus and having all the kids remark how wonderful he looks! But, I can easily imagine all the negative comments he will hear from fellow classmates while going to and from school.

The trouble comes not just from socializing, either. Negative comments from Johnny's teachers, or from other students when comparing grades, or his team losing at sports, or not having all the things the "cool" kids do – all these might also add to what Johnny believes about himself. And as we can see, most of these beliefs are trivial and have nothing to do with the reality of who and what Johnny is and can become.

When I was growing up, I was also exposed to negative experiences which often caused me to feel doubts and fears. On the other hand, my parents told me every day that "Silvas never quit," and this one empowering belief overrode negative influences I came across.

You only have to watch TV for a little while, and you will see the negative influences of discourtesy, rudeness, and anger to which children are constantly being exposed. From the fights on sitcoms, down to cartoon violence, it seems more and more popular for people to show each other rudeness rather than respect.

The great thing is that a martial arts environment can change this. It's not from the results of years of training that we can improve confidence, self-esteem and negative attitudes. *We can literally change negative behavior to positive actions in a matter of months by understanding the concept of building black belts from the inside out.*

To really grasp this concept, start by studying this illustration.

It has long been believed that if we build a student's self-confidence, he or she will give us more effort. The increased effort will produce results, and, in turn, increase the self-confidence. If this continued to raise the confidence level, effort and results would be the positive references a child needs to create a new positive belief system.

The challenge was that of all three; self-confidence, effort and results – self-confidence took the longest time to change. Many doubted me when I said the cycle really starts with results. However, *"results" is the only portion of the cycle that as an instructor*

I have immediate control over. Not only that, but I also have immediate control over the feelings and, therefore, the results of every student in the proximity of the student I am working to change.

In identifying results, much more is accomplished than me just looking at Johnny and saying "good job". It's true, that single compliment in itself is a positive reference that will help build his belief system, but using *a three-step system of praising* is much more powerful, and the impact much longer-lasting.

1. *Step One* is to be very specific about your praise. You are looking for two outcomes here. First, you want your student to gain a positive reference to influence his belief system. Secondly, you want to set a level of expectation in order to help the performance of the rest of the class as well.

2. *Step Two* is challenging the student to reach a higher level of performance while also painting a visual picture of how this action will dramatically improve his martial arts skills and self-esteem.

3. *Step Three* is tying all this down by showing true emotion to the student, to demonstrate my sincerity.

For illustration, suppose I just happened to catch Johnny punching with intensity and focus. I never let an opportunity like this go by because it goes back to doing the most productive thing possible at every given moment, and this is my opportunity right now to identify his progress and give him an iron-clad reference to high self-esteem and confidence.

"Johnny, I have to say I can't remember seeing you ever practice with such focus and intensity. I am so proud of you, and what you bring to our team! Would you like to take that up just a notch? Try exploding the next time I say 'punch.' Okay? I want you *done* the second I say punch. And, listen, that added speed will increase your power. Man, you are going to fly through that next stripe test! Did I tell you how proud I am of you? I did! Well, Johnny, *I mean it.*"

This is so powerful that you will immediately see an instant improvement in Johnny's level of confidence and effort. By setting such a high level of expectation, you will also see all the students in Johnny's proximity improve.

Becoming a "good-finder" and awarding proper praise is just one tool we have as instructors to make a huge impact on confidence and all the other character traits that are necessary to build our future black belts. In upcoming chapters, we will examine Training Incentive Programs, Curriculum, Building Trust, Social Atmosphere, Phase Training, Promotions, and Wants vs. Needs.

Just remember to do the most productive thing possible at every given moment.

CHAPTER TWO

IT'S NOT WHAT YOU TEACH, IT'S HOW YOU TEACH IT THAT'S IMPORTANT

WHY DID I NEED to come up with my *Solution*? Because, like most of us, I had some business problems and school challenges.

I kept thinking about the basics. Traditional martial arts were for warfare and self-defense, but, also, there is a huge attraction for children to get involved. So something has to give. I remember how, when I came up in the arts, I was expected to learn 240 self-defense techniques and 20 forms!

Learning complicated forms and difficult training patterns takes time and lots of practice. On the other hand, children have homework and a social life, not to mention other sports and hobbies that take up their time.

And yet, in our schools, so much depends on the kids being able to learn forms and patterns as fast as possible.

For example, the Training Incentive Program, or TIP testing, requires students pass monthly stripe testing exams. Two weeks are for learning, one week for review, and then its test time. If you are going to use this program as a positive tool, then all students should be able to grasp the material and pass the test.

If you run a great school, you will attract lots of students. Teaching fifty or more children in a class requires plenty of skill; however, teaching should also be fun.

Now, after watching many schools teaching many styles, it came to my attention that *instructors were more concerned with students memorizing material than performing material.* And I kept thinking, "martial arts isn't about memorizing, but rather performing like a champion, with power, speed, focus, accuracy, intensity, and excellence".

So I asked myself, "Why is it a child can play a video game for hours on end, but gets bored in school – even at a martial arts school?"

And this question led me to discover the *Solution.*

The *Solution* came to me in the most unlikely location. I was sitting in my car at a traffic light in Ft. Lauderdale, Florida, listening to a Tony Robbins tape. Tony was talking about changing your state of mind and creating emotion, so he had you do an exercise. First, Tony did caution that, if you were in a car in traffic, you might attract a little attention, but I played along anyway.

Tony had you hold your hands six inches apart and clap. Then, he wanted you to stretch your hands at arm's length and clap. To do this, I had to roll down the windows, and, yes, I soon discovered what he meant by attracting attention.

But the point of this exercise was that, *"motion creates emotion"*. Small movements make you feel confined, but the large motion creates energy and a feeling of excitement. Tony also challenged you to look in a mirror, stand tall with your arms overhead like a victory award, and *not* smile.

Suddenly, at that moment, it became clear to me why my traditional forms were not exciting. *There were no long moves.* For example, our beginning forms were designed to teach students to block while retreating, and they started off with eight blocks that were all small moves. There wasn't anything in our forms or patterns that induced a feeling of power by creating energy and emotion. So I decided to incorporate that "long move" concept in drills and forms of my own design which, above all, would create energy.

I used my own children as a test by creating new forms for them to practice. Turns out, they loved doing the new forms, and picked them up fast. But, the neat thing is that when they performed them at the school, all the other kids wanted to learn them also. And, these experimental forms were not just thrown together. When designing them, I kept in mind all the challenges of teaching "video game generation" students.

For example, I mentioned that students don't have a lot of practice time, and they need to learn the forms quickly. So, I started thinking about how kids memorize their phone numbers. They don't memorize ten digits in one block, but rather the area code, first, then the prefix, and then four digits. Much easier!

So, when designing my forms, there were the first three moves, the next three moves and, finally, the last four moves. Each of these sections was taught on a monthly basis as a requirement for TIP testing. This accomplished several good things. *Even very young students could easily memorize these sets of moves. They could be performed with the qualities of a champion for TIP testing; and the instructor could accomplish all this while having fun teaching.*

The new moves were all long and powerful, in line with what I had learned from Tony Robbins, "motion creates emotion". Since I wanted high-energy classes, the easiest way to make this happen was to design a curriculum that automatically gave me the desired results. I even went a step further by ending the new beginning form with the student standing tall, arms held high in a victory pose. (It really *is* hard to stand like that without smiling.) The student looked and felt great. I even had the student say "Victory!" while striking the pose. The results were amazing – great energy, high-performing students, and easy classes to teach.

But that was just the start of developing what I took to calling my "Universal Curriculum". I used this name because the moves were "universal" to most martial arts. The punches, blocks and kicks were already practiced in just about every style, although, naturally, they may have different names or titles attached. Having this in common was another important goal since I consult with so many schools representing so many different arts, systems and styles.

My planning became a little more detailed. Difficult kicks were done on the right leg since most kids were right-handed. The forms were short, but each one was designed to be linked with all the others, meaning that an intermediate student could link together three or four forms for competitive purposes. But, above all else, *the most important thing is that the forms had the "video game" addiction built in.*

Ask yourself the same questions I did. "Why is it that kids can play video games for hours? Why do kids love MTV? Why is it that kids get fidgety in a school classroom?"

My answers? Video games offer immediate feedback. You, the gamer, are either progressing through the levels, or you lose. But, the important thing is that you understand what you did right, or what you did wrong, so you can progress to the next level. Once there, you are challenged all over again. It's not as easy as the previous level; and kids love this constant sense of being challenged, when thing happen and change fast. Just like on MTV, where the longest scene in a music video is four seconds.

By now, I am sure you can easily figure out why kids can't sit still in school. But, my forms were fast-moving. The sequence was natural, so students got immediate feedback if the form was correct or not. All the moves done in the forms were part of the warm-ups and "drills for skills"; therefore, students could easily correct themselves. *Most importantly, I had both a basic form and more advanced moves for those students who were ready for the next level.*

This was the "video game" concept of challenging. The basic form may have had a sidekick, but, if the student mastered that quickly, I would challenge him or her to insert a three-kick combination to take the form to a higher level. This not only kept interest up but also gave the students an incentive for constant improvement.

This concept is solid, and it's a valid solution for all the challenges I mentioned at the beginning of the chapter. However, there is also the important question of keeping faith with tradition. Let's discuss tradition for a second, and then get back to what's really important.

Here's a story I like to tell. A family was getting together for a holiday dinner, and the kids were helping mom prepare the traditional ham. Their mother took the ham out and cut a couple of inches off the thin end.

The kids asked why she did that, and mom replied, "I learned how to cook a ham from my mother. She always cut it this way, but... *hmm,* why don't we ask her?"

They went to the other room and asked grandmother, "Why do you cut the small end of the ham?"

"Why, that's how my mother taught me. *Hmm,* Let's give great-grandma a call and ask her."

They got great grandma on the phone. "Why is it you always cut a couple of inches off a ham before cooking it?"

"That's easy," Great-grandma answered. "I had a very small pan, and that's the only way I could fit the ham into the pan."

Okay, sure, maybe your particular style of martial arts has a better reason for its traditions. But did you ever wonder why your forms may have three steps and then change direction? *Could it possibly be the founder had a very small room and could only move three steps in each direction?*

My point here is that times are changing, and so is the market for our various arts. I feel it's more important to keep our students interested, to build up their confidence and self-esteem, and then later on we can eventually teach them all the traditions.

I had this same discussion back in 1989 with the pioneering American Kenpo Grandmaster, Ed Parker. As is also traditional, I asked the grandmaster's permission to establish a creative curriculum for kids. I explained my concept about teaching students from the inside out and got his blessing. The results were that I taught a single school with 1,300 students while the average Kenpo school had 100 students. I also promoted hundreds of children to black belt who, yes, went on to learn traditional Kenpo.

So I seemed to have discovered that it's not what you teach, but how you teach it that's truly important. At least, this is what I originally thought. Now, in the next chapter, we will explore an improved version of this same concept; "It's not *what* you teach, or *how* you teach, but rather *how you make your students feel*, that's important."

In fact, that's the "main thing".

It's important to remember that the "main thing" is to keep the "main thing", the "main thing".

CHAPTER THREE

Classroom Mechanics: It's Not About You – It's All About Them

IT'S NOT WHAT YOU TEACH, or how you teach it, but, rather, how you make them feel, that is the key. To do this, it's important we know why students take lessons. We are in the service business, after all, and if we are going to help people change their lives for the better through martial arts, we must provide the solutions to all their challenges.

So why do people take martial arts? I believe everyone studies the arts for the same reason. However, doing a seminar, when I ask this question, I get all sorts of answers. Many people say students come to them for self-defense, others say fitness, self-confidence, social environment and – instructors often cringe when someone says – "just for an activity". Why the cringing? Because, as an instructor, martial arts is your way of life; however, until students experience the arts long-term, they may not realize the special joy and value of our way of life.

So, once again, the question is, "*why do people take martial arts?*"

Think about it. If students come to you for self-defense and, after several months, they learn some effective techniques, then they will understand how to evaluate their environment and defend against possible threats. How do they feel? Good. Their new self-confidence makes them feel good, and, what about students who want fitness? In a few months, they lose 20 pounds and look at themselves in the mirror. What happens? They feel good.

I could go on and on, but now you see what I'm saying. S*tudents all come to you for the same reason. They seek to feel better about themselves. They want to feel good.* That's why I point out that it's not about you or your art, it's totally about them.

Okay, I hear you. I understand that we can't sellout and become a fun factory. We need to pass along the values of the arts. True, but this book is about making a difference in many lives and helping thousands of students. As an instructor, you face plenty of challenges, so how can my *Solution* help you? How can we really make all our students feel good and teach great martial arts at the same time?

For example, If a student is misbehaving, you need to exert discipline. However, that's not building a black belt from the inside out. We actually need to instill *self-discipline*, so we don't have to yell or put our foot down.

If I have to motivate a class over and over again, somehow along the way I didn't communicate the point of martial arts. What I should have done is teach self-motivation, if I was building this particular student from the inside out. And this is not a complicated process; you just need to disguise these lessons in self-control through the mechanics of your classroom. *Something magical occurs when you understand "state management" and appreciate the student's desire to rise to the level of the instructor's expectations.*

Let's looks at some of the challenges we face in classes. Certain students lack enthusiasm, and you take it personally. There is always that one student who does a move with the wrong foot. Why does it never fail that a couple of students need discipline? *It's gotta be the phase of the moon!* What other explanation could there be for so many kids not concentrating, right?

I feel your pain, so the following "Classroom Mechanics" outline a "ten-step" system for class planning that will result in dynamic classes, automatic motivation, class variety, martial arts education, great protocol, happy motivated instructors, and great students.

CLASSROOM MECHANICS

1. *You need to start strong.* In fact, it should be your goal to get students at a level-ten, emotionally, before they throw their first kick or punch. Teaching motivated students is fun. The energy is high, and the students are eager to learn. Why not start your class with something that automatically induces this state in the students? When you say, "Line up!" students should run to their positions, clap their hands, yell and high-five each other. Why? "*Mo-*

tion creates emotion". The mere act of a dynamic line-up induces a state of energy and excitement.

2. The line-up needs to be immediately followed by putting students in a *powerful stance;* shoulders back, head high, reciting the student pledge, or making positive affirmations. This "power position" creates a feeling of energy, and speaking out in a loud, strong, voice creates confidence. This effect is the backbone of "state management". *Our physiology dictates our mental state.* Stand like you are depressed, head low and chest hollow, and you will feel depressed. Stand strong and you feel powerful.

3. Now it's your turn, as the instructor, to "sell the class" or "preframe". It's no different than turning on a TV show and seeing the previews. This 30 seconds makes students happy to be there and looking forward with anticipation to the next 45 minutes.

Example: "Class, you are going to be glad you came today. Our lesson is about gaining power. We are not going to have to do a thousand pushups or lift weights. Instead, I am going to share with you how, just by understanding the principles of height, width, depth, and the proper application, you will double your power in the next 45 minutes. Raise your hand if that sounds good to you. Great! Let's get started!"

4. *Warm-Ups.* This is always such an important part of class; however, in most cases, it is either overlooked or poorly planned. If the warm-up is not

motivating, exciting, and empowering, all the energy you just created in the first part of the class will be lost.

Why is this important? First of all, kids just plain need to exercise. Our school systems no longer offer fitness. Afterschool "activities" have become time to play video games, and children are getting to be overweight and out of shape. So, if you design a creative warm-up, you will excite your students, challenge them, develop confidence, and also really and truly make them feel good through the production of endorphins, which are a natural byproduct of exercise.

The warm-up should be a combination of aerobics, strengthening, core training, and flexibility. Exercises should be age-appropriate, so kids can do the exercises correctly, and the instructor needs to coach and motivate the children to put forth their best effort. Variety is important; there are literally hundreds of exercises, and no two classes should ever be the same.

5. *Drills for Skills.* These are drills you do in order to develop one particular quality of a champion. Overall, there are *six championship qualities: power, focus, accuracy, intensity, excellence and speed.* A great martial artist needs all six to achieve a tip-top performance.

About ten years ago, Paul Garcia, one of my instructors, was doing stripe testing. He kept a student after class and mentioned his kata was good but lacked power. We scheduled a retest for the following day. The performance was the same, and once more Paul asked the student to repeat the kata. Again - same results.

Paul questioned the student. "I need to see more power."

The child answered, "I am yelling as loud as I can!"

The student related power to the kiai. We, on the other hand, were relating power to velocity, body alignment, penetration, rotation and back-up mass. It was then I decided the *Solution* was to create a portion of class that taught the six qualities of a champion – excellence is about more than just repetitions of kicking and punching, but, rather, involves the science behind the art.

6. *Walk the lines.* In a classroom, students form lines. One of the best things an instructor can do is not to stand in the front of the class but, instead, "walk the lines". This causes the instructor to get in close proximity with all the students, thereby making them feel they are getting private attention in this group atmosphere. It also gives you the opportunity to provide positive feedback, which enhances every student's experience.

7. *Life Skills.* Use opportunities of becoming a good-finder to teach life skills. By noticing when a student shows great focus and remarking on it, you will get repeated good behavior from that student as well as others. Remember how I said in the beginning of this chapter that students want to please their instructor by rising to the instructor's level of expectations?

Suppose you tell a student, "David, you are displaying great focus. There is a lot going on in this class, but your eyes are focused, you are concentrating, and I have to tell you, it's that type of intense focus that will not only make you a great martial artist, but also a great student in school. Nice job, sir."

A lot of things will immediately happen by doing this. Keep in mind, it's not about you disciplining students; it's about their building up self-discipline. By becoming a good-finder and identifying either benefits or a well-performed action, you will immediately transform the entire class.

    8. Motivation is the KEY. Create emotion by becoming animated. As the instructor and coach in your class, you are the leader and set the tone. *Your students will not be more motivated than you are.* Knowing this, there are several tools we can use to become lively and, thus, more motivating to the students.

Simple keys are; Clap when you are calling repetitions or doing drills. Walk briskly around the room and create movements that coincide with your commands. For example, if you want students to do something faster, snap your fingers. Want it louder? Ask for it and cup your ear while leaning towards the class. Looking for excitement? Use your voice. You need to be loud. Want to make a point and be sincere? Lower your voice, but speak with passion.

I had an instructor, Eddie Diaz, from Texas. He was so good at becoming an animated instructor that one day he lost his voice. No problem. Just through his gestures alone, the students knew exactly what he wanted them to perform. This later became a regular feature of the class, since it taught students to focus and to pay attention. And parents became amazed at their children's ability to concentrate and follow directions without a word being said.

9. *Have a critical eye.* It is important, while leading a class, that you can immediately identify a student having trouble meeting a challenge or who is doing a move wrong. *Nothing gets a parent more upset than seeing their child not getting the proper attention.* However, it's not necessary to point out an individual child. The right thing to do is to simply reset the goal by explaining all over again what you want. It may be necessary to walk the lines and get in close proximity with the child who is having the challenge. Some children are kinesthetic learners, and so, at times, you will need some hands-on teaching.

Again, the point here is to not let incorrect behavior continue but to have the tools to make the correction, in order to get good behavior without singling out a student and making them feel uncomfortable.

10. The final Classroom Mechanic is *"listening positions".* When I conduct instructor training, I always get comments like, "What about the kid who won't sit still?" Or, "How do I stop my students from chewing on their belts?" These, again, are discipline problems, and our goal is to build our students from the inside out. We don't want to discipline - we want happy students who behave well and excel. Listening positions focus the stu-

dents' bodies so they can focus their eyes on you and have the ability to concentrate.

For example, if you are doing a lengthy talk, have students "lock it up". They sit down, legs crossed, hands on knees, back straight, chin up and breathing deeply but quietly. This is a great focus position and will solve the "eating the belt" challenge as well as the problem of too much moving around. Be sure to constantly acknowledge students who are sitting perfectly so that others will follow suit, and in this way, you will get repeated good behavior.

For a short correction, students can "take a knee". They simply put one knee down with both hands on the knee, back straight and looking forward. And, for a quick talk, have them in a rest stance; legs shoulder-wide and hands clasped behind the back. The goal is to have your students display self-discipline. After all, we started off this chapter by saying, "it's how you make your students feel that is important".

By creating a dynamic classroom that automatically instills good behavior and helps make great students, even your younger ones will leave a training session with a sense of pride and encouragement.

Next up is "The After-Class Checklist."

The goal here is retention, preventing challenges, and creating loyal students for life.

CHAPTER FOUR

THE AFTER-CLASS CHECKLIST

OKAY, NOW BEFORE YOU start to think I lost my train of thought, I need to relate a true story. I believe it will help explain why the After Class Checklist truly relates to building students from the inside out.

We finished class at East West Karate one day, and one of my instructors, Paul Garcia, was watching a student outside near the walkway. This student would not be classified as one of our most enthusiastic students. In fact, you would probably consider him a "C" student. (If you are not familiar with "A", "B" or "C" students, a "C" student soon becomes a "See Ya" student because he has one foot out the door already.)

Paul walked out front and sat down next to the student and began a conversation. Paul discovered that Eric's mom worked and had to leave her job really fast to pick him up from class, so he needed to sit on the curb and be ready when she arrived. Paul asked him how he enjoyed class.

"It's okay," Eric answered.

Paul then asked, "What other sports do you like?"

"Skateboarding is my favorite. I can do this, and I can do that."

Paul took a good ten minutes building a relationship with Eric by taking a true interest in what Eric liked to do outside of martial arts. This is a great point to remember: *"You become interesting only after you become interested in the other person."*

In other words, Paul Garcia, at that time, was the National American Sport Karate Association (NASKA) middle-weight champion and a member of world famous *Team Paul Mitchell*. He could have tried to impress Eric with these facts. However, Paul wanted to build a relationship with Eric, so he became a listener, instead.

There's another good saying for us to remember: *"God gave you two ears and one mouth because he wanted you to listen twice as much as you talk."*

"Interesting, because interested" and "listen twice as much" – commit to either of these ideas as habits, and you will see great changes in your life.

Next time Eric was in class, Paul was teaching a technique and wanted students to improve their balance.

"Hey, Eric, I hear you are a great skateboarder. Can you do me a favor and come to the front of the class. When you are doing tricks on your skateboard, and it's getting pretty fast and tough, how do you get better balance? Would you show us?"

Eric, now smiling from ear to ear, said, "You gotta bend your knees and get lower, just like the horse stance."

Paul thanked Eric for sharing his expertise with the class.

You can probably already guess what happened. *Right!* The relationship Paul built in ten minutes was a crucial technique for building a student from the inside out. The trust and respect that began out on the sidewalk, then manifested in class, and became the turning point for this student. Paul could now ask more, challenge more and expect more from Eric's performance because, almost overnight, Eric had found his confidence and believed in himself like never before. He was now ready to get out of that comfort zone and move forward.

Well, okay, you might decide my "end of class" techniques are obvious solutions to common problems. However, let me tell you this much. I visit schools on a consistent basis in three nations, and I very rarely see all these systems put to use.

End of class strategies will improve attendance, build value and create anticipation for the next class. You will also re-educate the parents on the value of your program. More importantly, you will have the opportunity to enhance your personal relationship with mom and dad. This is invaluable if their child ever loses motivation, or if there are any parental concerns in the future.

Once you have finished your cool-down, it's now time to build up some anticipation for the next class. Here is a technique used on TV shows all the time. Before signing-off, most TV shows will "tease" viewers with preview highlights of the next episode. This creates anticipation; and you feel like just can't miss the show the following week!

In our martial arts schools, we should be doing two things during cool-down time. One: create a vivid picture in the students' minds of all they will be learning and all the fun they will be having in the next class. Two: tell them why it's so important to attend by relating the class to the upcoming stripe test or evaluation. Remind them of the short amount of time before the next progress test and about how attendance and performance is tied into that.

I use a technique I termed "Ya Gotta Be Here". Without getting into the strategies of the TRAINING INCENTIVE PROGRAM (TIP) testing, it's important for right now that you understand that each month every student in your school should be tested for a stripe on their belt. This is one of the keys to teaching students goal setting as well as your chance to give each student a well deserved pat on the back.

Okay, let's imagine that we have just finished stripe testing. My "Ya Gotta Be Here" speech would go something like this:

"I just want to congratulate everyone on a job well done. That stripe on your belt is more than a piece of electrical tape. It is a sign that you have made progress towards your next goal. It signifies that you have attended class, made progress, did hundreds of kicks and hundreds of punches. You could have sat around the house like many kids, but you did something positive. You applied yourself to a worthwhile goal that will help every aspect of your life. You shouldn't walk in the door tonight. No. When you get home you should *glide on air* – that's how proud you should be of yourself."

"Now when we succeed at a goal, we should do two things. First, celebrate! So, give yourself a big hand and a pat on the back. Second, we need to reset a new goal.

Now next week *you gotta be here*. That is the week we will learn the first part of the material for your next stripe. So where do you have to be next week? That's right! Be here for two classes."

Okay, let's jump ahead in time. We are finishing classes after the next week. The speech I make then goes like this:

"Great work today. Now next week I need to have you here in class. We are learning the second part of the material for stripe testing. Stripe testing is only three weeks away so, please, *you gotta be here* next week."

And the following week, you wrap up teaching the new material:

"Okay, class when we take the stripe test in two weeks, it's more than just memorizing new material. I also want to see improvement on what you learned in the past. Next week is review week. *You gotta be here* for that. We will review both your new and old material. Remember, stripe testing is in just two weeks."

Jump forward. You are now one week out: "Congratulations, class! I think we are ready to stripe test next week. Just one more thing. *You gotta be here* twice next week. Monday and Tuesday we will be pre-testing, and then, the rest of the week, its stripe testing again. Please, make sure you are on time and ready."

You will be discovering that the purpose for each class is to prepare the students to successfully pass their stripe test. These constant weekly reminders assure our students will be in class and are preparing for their next celebration over meeting their goal.

The next part of our "end of class" strategies is to remind our students about what we did today.

Now, you might be thinking, "What a waste of time! Why would we do that?" Think about this: If you asked a child, "what did they learn new in school", how would most answer?

"Nothing."

Our students' parents are paying a good price for tuition. The last thing I want is a student getting in the car, or arriving home, and to have a parent ask, "How was martial arts? What did you learn new?", and have the student answer, "Nothing."

Therefore, my solution is to tell the students in 30 seconds what they learned new in class today, and to remind them of how much fun they had. If you have ever given a public speech, you already have done this. Because, in preparing a speech, you first tell the audience what you are going to talk about. You then talk about it, and finally wrap it up by telling them what you've talked about. Same thing with the class. We sell the anticipation of the class and explain to them what they will be learning. We then teach the class, and, finally, we remind them of what they learned, and why it was so important that they attended.

Now you are ready to bow the class out. No, I didn't forget announcements; I just don't see the point of dragging the class down with a list of upcoming events. From the student's point of view, it is way more important he or she leaves while still excited, sweaty, and smiling from ear to ear. I mean, do you really think the child is going to run home and shout out, "Mom, the instructor wanted to remind you of these four upcoming events, time and dates!"

There are much more effective ways of communicating this kind of information. With parents having such busy schedules, you should not limit yourself to only one way, either, but rather use several sources of information, including handing out a calendar of events in your monthly student newsletter. You would also do well to have an event schedule in your school. Nowadays, many schools are using a flat-screen TV to set up a professional slideshow of announcements. Others send out weekly e-mail announcements along with a motivational message or inspirational story. This is a great way to show parents and students you are thinking about them on the weekends. Schools that have gone hi-tech can text message to cell phones and use a service like *Phone Tree* for automatic voice-message delivery. Anyway, the real point here is not to waste time in class or cause unproductive downtime when there are easier and more effective communication methods available to you.

When the class is bowing out, *your team should be in their Strategic Stations.* One instructor remains on the mat. He is offering extra help as well as prepping the next class. Another instructor is stationed over by the parents, building rapport and fielding questions and concerns. A third team member is manning the front door.

This last one is a very important station because he or she does more than greet incoming student and say good-bye to exiting students. This person should be an expert at reading body language. It is this person's job to make sure everyone is happy. The last thing we want is a student leaving who may have just had a problem with another student in the locker room. Or a student leaving, and we forgot to give the extra help we promised.

It's also important to watch students arrive. We make sure that if a student is coming in the door but looks like he would rather be home playing, we intercept that student and talk a little bit, to make sure everything is alright, and the student is motivated.

As you can see, there is more to planning a class than deciding what punches, kicks and drills to do. When you consider the dynamics that are involved in a class, and the complexity in developing the relationships, excitement and emotions to build our students from the inside out, you can appreciate the systems and solutions we employ.

In our next chapter, we will discuss "teaching benefits". I coined this phrase in the early '90s when I began teaching others my own teaching methods. However, this concept has grown by leaps and bounds, since that time, into an easy-to-apply system that will change your classes and students forever.

"To hear is to doubt, to see is to be deceived, but to feel is to believe." Ed Parker

CHAPTER FIVE

THE BENEFIT DRIVEN SCHOOL

IN AUGUST OF 1989, I had just opened my school in Coral Springs, Florida. Even during the grand opening, I was still having some finishing touches done to the interior. One of the walls was being painted with a huge mural of clouds on which were written out all the "benefits" martial arts schools say that they pass on to their students: self-confidence, honesty, perseverance, patience, respect, courage, and self-esteem.

These were "Benefits" or "Life Skills" that we promoted in our advertising material, the very same promises we made to new students who joined my school. I felt that once they were up there on the wall, I had an even bigger responsibility to make sure my students gained these skills as fast as possible – for two reasons.

One: As I explained earlier, these benefits and skills are the goals of building black belts from the inside out. Two: I also knew they were values and attributes lacking in society and the public school system; and if martial arts was really going to make a difference in a student's academic and business career, they were what I needed to base my school on.

While I was teaching a class one evening, my artist was also there, painting the mural on the wall. At this time, I had maybe ten students, and I was truly a one-man show. After teaching a class for a whopping *two* students, the artist and I began to talk.

He said to me, "If you keep teaching like that, and changing kids' lives, you will never have to worry about filling this school with students or making a great living. People will just tell other people, and you will do great."

He must have been right because, in the first year, I enrolled 500 students, and two years later, Greg Silva's East West was the largest single school in the U.S., with over 1,200 active students. No brag. Just fact.

I recently read an article by Zig Ziglar where he talked about how successful companies go about hiring employees. He wrote, "There have been many research studies done on what employers are looking for in an ideal employee. The one I often quote found that 85% of the reason a person gets a job and then gets ahead in that job is due to attitude, and only 15% is due to a technical skill. Employers are looking for someone who is willing to get the job done... and get it done without complaining or griping."

If you don't believe yet in the value of a benefit driven martial arts school, take a second, and let's see what others have to say.

December 7, 2006 *Dallas Morning News*: "Many employers say the moral and ethical lessons that are taught along with the academic curriculum at faith-based schools better equip graduates to become valued employees."

December 10, 2005 *Dallas Morning News:* "What I hear from the business people I'm dealing with is that ethics and corporate responsibility are absolutely at the top of their list when searching for new employees," says Frank Lazarus, President of the University of Dallas.

"There was a time when the three r's were shorthand for readin', 'ritin' and 'rithmetic, but those letters take on a new meaning today. Respect, reverence and responsibility are the three r's we stress for our students," says Rosemary Seltzer, Principal of a 425-student K-8 school.

If all of this is true in the business community, you can be sure it is also true for children and their academics. In Coral Springs, several years after introducing "teaching benefits" and "life skills" to my martial arts students, something amazing happened. Out of the three high schools in town, *for six years in a row*, one of the valedictorians of one of the graduating class at each high school was a former or current East West Karate black belt.

Now, I understand, of course, that many of these children had very supportive parents; however, each of these high schools had more than 4,000 students, and I feel it is too much of a coincidence to say martial arts was not at least a small factor in their success.

So, how do we fulfill our promise to build all the wonderful benefits a martial arts school advertises? How do we make sure that students are empowered with these benefits and life skills?

I believe I have created three methods that not only a seasoned instructor can immediately put to use, but, more importantly, a system that even young, new instructors can easily adapt to their teaching skills.

The three methods are 1. Teaching Life Skills; 2. Experiencing Life Skills; and 3. Identifying Life Skills.

Teaching Life Skills is the most difficult of all three, but it has the greatest impact on our Little Champions, ages four to six. Since these children are so young, it may also be difficult for them to experience a benefit *without* getting upset or quitting. For example, if I want them to learn the lesson of disappointment in order to teach them about perseverance, they may get discouraged instead of understanding the meaning of the lesson and drill. You must always be careful to use drills that are age-appropriate both physically and mentally.

Teaching a life skill is just what it sounds like. You are spending a short amount of time telling or teaching your students what a certain benefit is, and how it relates to their experience in your class as well as at home or school. A little later in this chapter, I will go over *Opportunities to Teach Benefits*, and where and when to insert them into your classes.

Teaching a Benefit has three parts – *What, How, and Why?* If I were to teach respect to a four year old, I would first make sure I could do it in about 60 seconds because I would want them to get the message without having downtime or losing their attention in class. With my "What, How, and Why" plan in place, it might go something like this:

The What – "Class, one of the most important things about being a great black belt is showing someone respect. Respect it treating someone else like you like to be treated, or even better."

The How – "How we do that is to be aware of how people feel when they are around us. When you are nice to someone, you are treating them with respect. For example, if your mom asks you a question, you should answer 'Yes, m'am,' or 'No, m'am.' Being polite like this is respectful. It makes the other person feel good."

The Why – "The reason why this is so important is simply to make your friend, parent or teacher feel good. But as an added bonus, when you treat someone else with respect, they will also be nice to you."

Easy, right? Simply tell your class what the meaning of the life skill is in a way that is appropriate for their age. Next, explain how they can do this at your school or, more importantly, at home or academic school. And finally, tell how it's going to benefit them. The tie-in to homelife and academic schooling is very important. *We want to make sure that students are not just acting like black belts in our martial arts school but, rather, acting like black belts everywhere all the time.*

The term "acting like black belts" is very powerful. From day-one of training, a student is setting a goal to become a black belt; however, they don't have to wait three years to act like a black belt. Even the newest, youngest student can immediately start acting like a black belt.

This is the secret to a lot of any student's success. You may have heard the quote, "Fake it until you make it." Well, nothing is a better example than "acting like a black belt". You may not yet be empowered with respect at the beginning, but you can always act with respect, until it becomes a natural part of you.

Our next tool for instilling benefits is *"Experiencing Benefits"*. This is where you design a drill or class plan so the class gets to experience what the benefit "feels" like.

For example, let's say my goal is to teach the benefit of "Perseverance". I would then design a drill that tests the students' will to continue. In other words, get them to a point where they are probably going to feel like giving up or, at least, take a break.

One of my favorite ways is to use arm circles during my warm-up. In just a few minutes, the shoulder muscles begin to tire and burn. While doing the drill, I am motivating and encouraging the class; however, you can see it in their faces when they start to tire.

"Is anyone getting tired?"

Of course, they will say, "No!", so you continue.

"Does anyone want to give up?"

They will again say, "No!"

"Let me ask you a question. Is it alright to want to give up?"

Again, you will hear, "No!"

This is the beginning of the lesson. "Take a break, class. At times when things get tough, and you get a little tired, or you lose interest, it's natural to want to give up on something. No problem! That's okay. However, students that act like black belts understand the difference between wanting to give up, and using self-discipline and perseverance, instead."

"Not everything in life comes easy. You may have a problem in school, just like your parents may have a problem at work. The urge may come over you to give up or quit, but that is not the key to success or to achieving your goals. It's at this time when you need to dig down deep and keep trying, or, better yet, get some advice from your teacher, coach or parent."

"Hey, the best thing is that everyone in this class already proved to me you are not quitters! That last drill was tough, and you all hung in there. I'm proud of you. Next time you get that temptation to quit, think about this class, and the determination and perseverance you showed me."

"Experiencing Benefits" takes time because you not only need to design the drill, but also be able to articulate the lesson. Even so, the actual experience is the key to this lesson having an immediate and long-lasting impact on the student.

Our third tool for teaching benefits and life skill is to *"Identify Them"*. This is the easiest of all and can be used at any time throughout the class. The only challenge is that, as a teacher, most of us are always looking for things to teach or to correct. *The key to "Identifying Benefits" is to do just the opposite of teaching or correcting. Instead, always look to "catch" someone being good and doing something right.*

If you want to see what I mean by this, try doing a few pushups, and then ask your students or instructors to comment on them. Purposely do something a little wrong, and see what happens. I guarantee most of the comments you get will be on what you did wrong, even though you might have done eight out of ten perfectly.

Being a "good-finder" and catching someone doing something right takes a little practice. But, soon you will begin noticing everything. For instance, "Billy, would you please come to the front of the class. I've got to tell you what I see."

"You are really starting to act like a professional black belt. Your uniform is so clean, and your patches are perfect. Do you know what that tells me? You are taking pride in yourself. I can tell this by the way you are dressed. Pride leads to self-esteem, and people with self-esteem show great confidence. Class, can everyone please give Billy a hand."

Now, you may have started this paragraph by thinking it was a little silly to spotlight Billy simply because he had a nice, clean uniform; however, I hope you now understand how great Billy must be feeling, and how soon the rest of the class will start thinking more about their own appearance and the importance of feeling proud.

But wait, there's more. That was only part of the lesson. Remember, when working on benefits and life skills, we must always relate the lesson to outside the martial arts school. So, for example, something like this might be my next step.

"Class, I picked Billy, but many of you are showing me a new level of pride. In fact, I would bet that if I went to any one of your homes and inspected your bedrooms, I would see them super clean and neat."

You will hear some laughter now, most likely from the parents watching.

"Oh, oh! That's not good." Smile, but then get serious again. "Remember, we act like black belts in here and at home and at school. So I have an assignment tonight for you to practice your martial arts at home. But, you are not going to kick, block or punch. You are going to practice 'Pride' and 'Self-Esteem'."

"It may be that you will tidy up your room, or you could re-do a homework paper to make sure it is super-neat. You might ask mom or dad what you can do around the house. To be a black belt, we need to act like black belts. So tonight you are going to practice something really important that will eventually help you in your punching and kicking."

"Let me ask, if you take pride in everything you do, will your martial arts improve? You bet it will. Because, you are not going to settle for a low kick or a sloppy punch. You will practice with power and speed because you are proud of what you do."

You now have the tools to make some powerful changes in your students. I am sure you can see that creating beliefs will manifest itself in the physical standards of your students. Building from the inside out is the best way for high retention, drastic life changes, and super-performing black belts.

When do you teach these benefits? Benefits should be used as fast "bullet points" at any time throughout the class. You only spend 20 to 40 second at a time, to be sure your class stays action-packed. I have seen some classes concentrating so much on benefits, they seemed like a therapy session and not a martial arts class. So, keep things moving and use benefit training as a highlight.

By the way, there are two times during classes that are naturals for teaching benefits. The first comes after bowing-in, and the second, following the mat chat. I covered these areas in detail in the chapter about "Classroom Mechanics", but here is a quick reminder.

The class begins with a pledge or creed listing the tenets of a black belt. Then, during class, we should conduct a message or mat chat. Not only does this give the class a few minutes of rest, but it is also a good time for the instructor to pass on his wisdom by a brief lesson. Tying these lessons into something benefit driven is natural and should be part of each and every class.

CHAPTER SIX

WINNING-
OVER PARENTS

I BELIEVE TEACHING children martial arts is one of the happiest and most rewarding professions anyone can possibly have.

You actually witness, in a short amount of time, a shy, reserved child break out of his shell and turn into a leader. You see another child, one who was once sitting on the side-lines, now evolve into a punching-kicking machine, ready to take a key role in your demo team. And that formerly-chunky 8-year-old girl is now so proud of her accomplishments, she willingly takes on new challenges and is also setting some pretty intense goals of her own.

These are not just personal observations. When I conduct instructor training in any part of the world, I find a room full of black belt instructors who would agree. In fact, I hear the exact same words all the time - "I love teaching kids."

However, more often than not, that happy statement is followed up, in a different tone of voice, by - "It's the parents I have a hard time with."

Why is this? The kids are the students, you are the instructor, and the parents are just onlookers, right? So what's the big problem? As long as the child is learning, happy and training, you can build that future black belt from the inside out and be successful, right?

Wrong. Unfortunately, that is about as far from the truth as you can get. I say so because, it turns out, *kids don't quit martial arts - parents let them quit, want them to quit and often send a signal that will prompt the child to want to quit.*

The truth is if we are going to be successful in our goal of training black belts, we need to cultivate, educate, and win the support of the parents. In fact, this one job may well be your most important task when teaching martial arts to children. (Coaches of Little League, soccer, and other organized sports will also find this section of the book an invaluable tool.)

Why would a parent let their child quit a sport or any other healthy, wholesome educational activity such as martial arts? Remember how, at one time, they came to your school desperately seeking your help? Back then the issue might have been fitness, self-defense or confidence. They tried your program and saw value in what your mission was and trusted you to help get the job done.

What has changed?

The only reason why they would let their child quit is if they no longer appreciate the value or don't notice any progress towards the good results.

Why don't they notice results? One reason may be obvious. Are the parents of your students invited to see and hear what is going on in class? Too many schools have separate waiting rooms for parents or isolate the parents behind a viewing wall.

Once I visited a school in New Jersey where the owner had built a special room for parents with a small two-foot-by-two-foot window. It was almost as if the parents were caged; and here was this tiny, fast-food-style drive-up window that they would crowd around, trying to glimpse what was going on in the classroom.

I asked the instructor why he had built this special holding pen. His response was typical of many instructors - "the parents talk too much, they interfere with the class, correct their child, and... It just plain causes a distraction."

Eddie Diaz was the head instructor at our school in those days, and he and I were there to teach a few seminars and help the owner's staff with their classes. Now, Mr. Diaz has got to be one of the most dynamic children's instructors I have ever seen in action, and he just loved getting parents involved. Often there would be 30 kids in one of his classes, maybe 50 parents on the side, and the only person in the room you heard speaking was Mr. Diaz.

So, visiting this New Jersey school, Eddie felt uncomfortable about the parents being kept off in a private room. He would teach for a little while and then, for humor, walk over to this dinky little two-by-two fast-food-restaurant window and starting asking the parents for their "order"! And before the class was half-over, Mr. Diaz had invited the parents out onto the floor.

Soon Eddie had the class motivated and the parents captivated. Now they could see for themselves the progress being made and all of the great mental benefits he was teaching these children.

Involving the parents so they can view and hear the class is only the first step, however. Some parents will still want their kids to quit. If this is the case, you need to look at a few key areas of the class. For example, are you giving each child equal attention, or are you playing favorites?

When a parent is watching a class, the most important child in that class is theirs. If you are passing over their pride-and-joy to showcase your own favorite students, you are not building a relationship of trust with that parent. Even worse, if you are not noticing their child when they are doing something incorrectly, you are showing the parent that you do not care about their child's progress.

Just think about this for a second. Parents take pride in their child. Suppose a parent is watching class with all the other moms and dads. Can you imagine her leaning over to the parent next to her and saying, "See the little boy in the second row doing every thing wrong? *That's my boy.*" That would be crazy, right?

Now you can understand why, in this case, they not only let their children quit, but actually want them to. They will encourage him or her to try a different activity, and that kid soon becomes an ex-student.

So the lesson we are learning here is that it's of paramount importance parents get involved in the class. In this way, they can not only see the progress of their child's martial arts education, they are also reaffirming that they have been smart to choose your school. And, your school must be a great choice because you are giving their child your full attention and teaching with a critical eye, to make sure every students is learning correctly, so all the parents are proud of their children.

There are several other valuable teaching techniques that you can employ to make sure the parents stay involved and interested instead of becoming an annoyance.

The first technique is to assign the parents some responsibilities by giving them a role to play. For example, parents need to know that your school is all about having a positive attitude and passing out praise. When the kids perform, the parents should be keeping quiet out of respect for the instructor and the class. However, when it comes time to praise and encourage, parents should be applauding and participating in these shows of appreciation.

Here's a "for-instance". Suppose a group of kids have just learned a new form. You can get the kind of involvement you need by saying, "Parents, I am sure you agree with me that this form the kids learned today took a lot of concentration and hard work. I think these guys deserve a show of support. How about giving them a big hand?" Now you have involved the parent and, as an added bonus, your entire class is smiling and proud.

Another good technique is to use parents as pad holders when doing drills. First, of course, you need to give them a little education in how to hold the pads as well as how to coach and encourage the kids. Other parents who may go on watching can cheer everyone else along.

Once the parents get involved, you can take it another step farther by saying, "Parents, we did these drills on pads today because it helps the kids develop focus, accuracy and power. I would really like your children to practice at home for about ten or fifteen minutes on days when they don't come to class. And you can help by making it more fun. Hold these pads at home and have them do their kicks on both sides."

Okay, I can understand you might be worried that what I am really doing is teaching parents to be teachers; and sooner or later, they will be walking out on the floor, correcting their kids in class, or, worse, telling you when their kids should test or not! I admit this could happen – but only if your parents don't understand the proper etiquette and protocol.

Remember what we are trying to do. *We want to continually demonstrate the value of our school, and to do that we need the parents to be involved.* This must be the primary goal. In doing so, however, we also need to make sure the line between parent and teacher is never crossed. And, we insure this by educating the parents on the proper protocol of the martial arts.

As far as protocol goes, *what matters is that the parents adhere to the same rules as the kids do.* They, too, should bow into the school, refer to the instructor by his or her last name and respect classes by watching quietly. Instilling this good behavior and giving high-energy, upbeat classes are a sure cure for parental interference.

And, by the way, a time comes when you might want to talk to the parents about "letting go" by permitting their kids to take responsibility for themselves.

I recently visited a school and was sitting in the parent viewing area when a mom and a boy about eight-years-old arrived.

I said, "Hello. He looks excited about being here today."

"Yes," she said, "he was in his uniform ready for class early today. He loves sparring days." She then began to tie her son's belt.

"Wow," I thought, "this kid can tie his shoes but mom is tying his belt. *What about teaching him how to do it for himself?*"

Another example. We went to dinner with friends who have a ten-year-old son. The mom was talking about her child in school and was really upset at the school system. As a result, it seems she had ended up doing his homework for him.

Like many parents, it was more important that her child got a good grade, since it made her look better. That seemed more important than having her child learn responsibility. Dr. Robin Silverman refers to these as "helicopter parents" because they hover over their children in everything they do.

You can't change human nature, but you can change the behavior in your school. Parents are bringing their children to you for help; and we already know that black belts must be built from the inside out. So, if we are going to build confidence and true self-esteem, the kids need to believe they did it for themselves.

The truth is parents and kids need to experience failures as well as success. Parents should be told this fact of life during your graduations, in news letters and by other written material. Of course, every once in a while, one parent might slip back into "helicopter behavior". No problem. We just step into the office together and remind these back-sliders about our plans for helping their child accomplish his or her goals. And then we review the protocol.

I am sure I am not the only one who has dealt with the parent of a yellow belt who thought they knew more about running a martial arts school than me. In fact, every school has one. And, once they emerge, they don't mind telling you about all the stuff you are doing wrong!

What I am referring to are parents who bring up concerns they shouldn't be concerned about, who question what you are doing and make uninformed judgments about other students' rank and performance, etc. It is important that you accept this unhappy reality and properly prepare, so you are ready when things feel like they are going wrong.

Every time we received a complaint from a student's parent, my staff had a "five-step recovery system" they knew like the back of their hands.

The first step was to isolate the parent from the student and from the rest of the parents. "I understand you have a concern, Mrs. Johnson, and I would like to give this my full attention. Would you please step into my office?"

The next step is to listen carefully, let Mrs. Johnson get it all out of her system, before you try to justify anything. "Okay, I understand. Now is there anything else?"

Once Mrs. Johnson has finished, we want to express empathy using the "feel, felt, found technique".

"Mrs. Johnson, I feel I might not have fully explained the procedure for stripe testing. (You are showing that you are listening and take her concern seriously.) In fact, other parents have felt the same way in the past. (Mrs. Johnson is not alone, and you have handled this before − you're an expert.) "What we have found is that children should be awarded *only when they really earn something*. We have talked to a child psychologist about this, and if we are going to truly build your child's confidence, he needs to realize that it is up to him to work for things. We are fully prepared to help him reach the goal. I hope I can count on your support. I won't let you down."

This technique is great; however, you may have parents approach a junior instructor who is just not capable of handling the situation. In this case, you would go to the fourth step of the recovery system. We call it the "Iron Rule".

The instructor would tell Mrs. Johnson that he is unable to handle her concern; however, he will bring it to the attention of the manager, and we will have an answer in twenty-four hours.

The manager then takes the following steps: One, he or she will take responsibility, work out a practical solution for the challenge, fix the problem and convey the message to Mr. Johnson within twenty-four hours.

The fifth and final step is to send a "thank you" note to the complaining parent. "Mrs. Johnson, I sincerely want to thank you for bringing your problem to my attention. In doing so, I know that you are not only concerned about your son's situation but also for the well-being of our school. I truly hope we have found an acceptable solution. It is great to know we have the support of our students and their families. It is also important you know we have your best interests at heart."

Our last technique for winning over the parents is to educate them about not sending mixed signals to their children. By the way, I learned this lesson from Anita Fischler, a child psychologist who happened to be the parent of one of my students.

We met when I had just opened my school. She and two friends brought their four-year-olds to take a class. And, this happened way back in the early days when I needed every student I could get. Even so, during the first two classes, these kids were bouncing off the walls. I tried all the techniques I knew for teaching children, but they were just too young to handle a group class and get anything out of the program.

Finally, I ended up recommending that the four-year-olds wait six months and then come back. I explained how, for their children to get the most from our program, it needs to be a positive experience. I was concerned that I would spend so much time correcting the kids or disciplining them, they wouldn't enjoy the class and, instead of being positive, it might become a negative experience. I suggested they allow their children to start kindergarten, first, and then bring them back again in six months. I could tell they appreciated my frankness, and all the kids did return six months later.

Fours years down the road, two of the three received their black belts. During those four years, Dr. Fischler taught me a lot. One of the most profound lessons was why some kids quit.

You, too, have probably lost a student at one time or another and just could not understand why. He or she was always there, did great, was a budding superstar and all of a sudden... they quit. They quit, not because you did anything wrong – in fact, they may love the school. No, the chances are something happened on the home-front that sent a mixed signal which the child responded to.

For example, suppose your student is getting ready for class and overhears mom talking on the phone. "I would love to stop over, but Billy has martial arts class, and I need to drive him. Sometimes it seems like I am just a cab driver always taking him to class."

So, in an attempt to please his mom and make life easier for her, Billy announces he doesn't like martial arts and wants to quit. If this happens, and if you have failed to educate mom about all the positive benefits, she just might let him!

Or else, there is the case of mom and dad fighting. "Look at all these bills! Electricity, the car, insurance, karate!" Next thing, little Sara is saying she doesn't like class, in hopes her mom and dad will stop fighting.

These various scenarios can go on and on. The important point is to constantly educate parents so they understand that all kids have highs and lows in training. Explain to mom and dad that loss of interest is common, and you deal with it successfully on a regular basis. Your goal is to make sure their child develops all the benefits they are enrolled for, and to do that takes time, and there will naturally be some bumps along the way. Tell them about the great things you can accomplish together working as a team, and be sure, if a problem arises, that the parents will make you aware, so you can help.

Parents need to know they are a vital part of the team, if we are going to do our job and build their upcoming black belt from the inside out. Yes, many dynamics must fall into place, and it's a complex arrangement, to say the least. However, this chapter's techniques are proven ways to help along a few more students to their black belts, and will let you make a positive contribution to the lives of your young students. **Teaching children involves teaching parents, too.**

CHAPTER SEVEN

CURRICULUM INTEGRATION

DECIDING ON THE TITLE of this chapter was tough. My goals are to talk about various elements of disguised repetition; however, most of all, I don't want you to put my book down thinking you already know all about what that means.

There have been DVDs put out, seminars done, and magazine articles written on this vital subject of disguised repetition. I am not trying to insinuate that all these ideas aren't great for keeping downtime to a minimum, and entertaining students. Even so, this book is about building black belts from the inside out, so my concept is much larger than simply entertaining students through various clever new drills. To me, disguised repetition is really all about engaging the student's mind and getting amazing results in performance over a very short period of time. *My Solution is not so much about what we are doing, but why and how we do them.*

Keeping all that in mind, I was then going to title this chapter "Qualities of a Champion". Although developing the qualities of a champion is the underlying goal of disguised repetition, I once again felt that this approach limits itself by being mostly physical in nature.

By now I was thinking I'd just take the easy way out and refer to this chapter as the "Training Incentive

Program". The trouble is you would have definitely shut the book! How many TIP testing ideas have you already heard? And so that's when I finally had my "eureka moment", and the answer finally came to me. "Curriculum Integration", says it all.

"Curriculum Integration" sounds good and powerful – and it is. It encompasses the idea that everything will be tied together into a neat, yet dynamic package. It offers a way of combining many of the elements students need to be successful at whichever of your school's programs they happen to be enrolled in. So here's my tried-and-true approach to blending excellence in performance, disguised drill and those necessary qualities by which we as instructors judge the physical performance of our students.

Imagine this scenario. You are one among thirty students lined up in class, and the instructor is putting you through your paces. "Hey, if this is going to protect you on the street, you better put a little more power into it", says the instructor. "I like to see that technique done a little quicker. As Mr. Parker said, 'Those who hesitate will meditate in a horizontal position', so can I see a warrior face – PLEASE?"

All this time, you, the student, would love to please your instructor, but he or she is asking something more important of you and of the whole class. This instructor is really looking for Power Principles: for the students to become faster and to perform with greater intensity.

The challenge is, if you were really taking this class, you probably would have been doing a lot of grumbling to yourself. Questions and thoughts come up, like - "I'm doing it as hard as I can. What else do you want me to do? Faster – hey, I'm not you. *Warrior face?* What the heck are we doing here?" In other words, you, the student, are becoming increasingly frustrated and will soon begin to question if you have what it takes to make it to black belt. Not good.

To eliminate this frustration, to better educate and to make the class more entertaining, we are going to integrate the crucial elements of our curriculum. These elements consist, first, of our foundation – the core martial arts we are teaching – then, the Six Qualities of a Champion: Power, Speed, Focus, Accuracy, Intensity, and Excellence. And most importantly, we will also tie core curriculum and the Six Qualities into the school's goal system of testing for rank.

Your core material consists of the requirements your students must memorize: the self-defense, sparring drills, one-steps, and forms. And, the Six Qualities of a Champion define the standards of performance you want to see whenever the core material gets demonstrated. After all, martial arts are not a memory program, but an athletic sport, and self-defense art which need a high skill level to be able to either win the game or successfully defend ourselves.

Now, let's put it all together so you can more easily understand the practical applications. *Each month as you are teaching your core material, you concentrate on either a performance goal or on one of the Six Qualities.* The Training Incentive Program (TIP) is the method of goal-setting most modern schools use. It's the way contemporary operations break down the single, large goal of progressing from one belt to another by means of having shorter, monthly goals, in order to reward students and keep them on the right track. The method is to use a visual aid – a colored stripe on the belt – to build-in awareness of the Six Qualities.

Power – Blue Stripe. Symbolic of water. If you can't understand the relationship, just see what water did to make the Grand Canyon.

Focus – Black Strip. This relates to the color of the bulls-eye on a target.

Intensity – Red Stripe.

Speed – White Stripe. Our goal is to be as fast as lightning.

Accuracy – Green Stripe. Green represents growth; and, during this cycle, the students are learning how to understand and fine-tune the basics of the moves they are performing.

Excellence – Gold Stripe. The symbol of excellence in the Olympics.

For example, suppose a student begins a new cycle of belt testing; and let's assume he is learning a sidekick. The goal is to teach the mechanics, so he can correctly perform the move. Since instructors understand that repetition is the mother of skill, our student will be expected to practice the kick over and over again, until the move becomes a habit. At the same time, we must entertain the student, so he enjoys the repetition, even while we educate him and engage his thought process.

To do this, we set a two-fold goal for the first month. One: to learn the sidekick. Secondly: to earn a blue stripe in four weeks by demonstrating the kick with power.

We begin by explaining to the student what power is. It's more than just encouraging them to "hit hard". It's teaching them exactly what power is. Power is mass times velocity, or, more simply, weight times speed. Even though it moves slowly, a train is powerful because it is so heavy. A bullet is powerful, even though it weighs so little, because it travels so fast. In a sidekick, power comes from the speed of execution and the weight behind it.

A student right now, after learning what power is, can immediately begin to understand what mechanics it's going to take to develop a devastating sidekick. We then need our student to understand that he doesn't have to gain weigh to increase the mass behind the kick. He simply has to realize that moving his weight in one or a combination of all three dimensions will accomplish this goal. In other words, success comes from changing his height, depth or width. How does this happen with the human body? I can change my height by dropping down or lifting up. I can change my width by rotating. And I can change my depth by stepping or sliding.

So, once the student learns the basic kick, I can now begin teaching how to get more power by applying the fundamental principles outlined above. We will first increase the power by rotating our hips. Later on, we can increase the rotation by doing a spinning-sidekick. And, as for changing depth, we can add a shuffle or crossover step. We can then teach the student how, if he chambers high and kicks down towards the target while dropping his height, impact is added. The result? Our student is at all times learning to kick, but, more importantly, he is also being mentally stimulated through a growing understanding of the physical concepts, all while getting entertained by doing the kick differently and better.

To keep on taking the training up to new levels, more power principles are added throughout the month. These may include: *Penetration* – the concept of not just meeting our target but following through or penetrating the target. *Surface Contact* – the reason a pin easily penetrates the surface is because it's so small. In a sidekick, making contact with just the heel creates more power – you can imagine the difference between getting sidekicked with a flat heel or by a woman in high heels!

Another principle of power is to borrow the force from your opponent. In other words, more power is transferred, in the form of impact, if an opponent is moving towards you as you time your kick – just as a car would be damaged more if it hit another car head on. A similar principle is to create more power by taking advantage of bracing. This applies if your opponent is up against something, or is braced, and can't move backward when hit.

I can go on and on about teaching and developing the qualities of a champion, however, that is not the point of this book. The concept I am trying to drive home in this chapter can be summed up with a short story my instructor, Ed Parker, used to tell at his seminars.

By the way, Mr. Parker knew better that anyone else the importance of teaching students from the inside out.

He understood that, if his art of Kenpo was to keep growing long after he was gone, it could only happen in one way. Kenpo would have to self-perpetuate because his students gained the ability to learn and grow without anyone's help.

So Mr. Parker's seminar story is about this young executive who had bought an outdoor grill and was home with the box open, his toolkit nearby, and what seemed like 100 parts spread across the patio. Struggling to make sense of the directions, he soon became frustrated and gave up and called on his neighbor, "Sam, The Fix-It Man."

Sam came over, and the young executive complained long and loud before finally asking Sam if he could put the barbeque grill together for him.

Sam pushed the directions aside, and in a short time, had correctly assembled all the pieces.

The executive look at Sam in amazement. "I've been trying to put that darn thing together for an hour. You come over, don't even look at the directions, and assemble it in twenty minutes! I don't understand Sam, how you could do that without once looking at the directions?"

"Well, boss", Sam explained with a smile, "you see, I can't read and, when you can't read, *you've got to think.*"

My point here has everything to do with teaching students from the inside out. If we build-in the life skills and, at the same time, educate students as to why they do something – not just teach them how to do it – a truly amazing thing happens. Students not only find the classes more fun and more interesting, **they also become black belts instead of just "getting a black belt."**

CHAPTER EIGHT

It's Becoming Clear

AS WE ADD PIECES to the puzzle, we begin to see how each new piece falls into place. With each new piece, we begin to recognize the big picture. When doing a jig-saw puzzle, we first do the outside pieces, the frame. These squared-off outside pieces are the most obvious and easiest to find.

For years, martial artists believed that martial arts training built confidence and perseverance. So, for years, the outside pieces suggested that if a parent were looking to develop these qualities in their child, you would have the child enroll for lessons, and three years later, he or she would earn their black belt and be fixed. Don't misunderstand. I am not suggesting that training doesn't enhance life skills or values; however, it is my opinion that, for a student to endure three years of training, they would have to already be fairly confident, patient and determined.

I remember back in the 70's when you could walk into almost any martial arts schools, and you would see a poster that read something like this...

Your Sensei is one-in-ten-thousand
10,000 people will start training in the martial arts
After three months 5000 will quit
A year later only 500 will be left
After three years two will make it to black belt
Only one will become a Sensei
Your Sensei is literally one-in-ten-thousand

It is my guess that these two black belts must have been pretty determined and very tough-skinned to make it!

It is this poster that convinced me, if we were going to use martial arts to help people, if we were going to really make a difference in peoples' lives, we first had to examine the character of those who made it to black belt and find a way to develop those same qualities in our white belts. If we did that, we should be able to significantly increase our success rate in helping people as well as increase the number of people who would succeed in their training and become black belts.

Understanding this is one thing; however, developing a system to make these changes happen is another. Not only do we need a system for changing attitudes and beliefs, we need to do it *quickly*.

This is not only my rule but also what our culture and society demands. Americans are used to having things done fast. From fast-food to instant information on the internet to on-demand TV, people are looking for immediate results. More importantly, kids born since the mid-to-late '80s have grown up with computer games, music videos and TV shows that create ever-shorter attention spans. The "MTV Generation" demands quick thinking and faster decision-making. It's very difficult to convince people to be patient when they are not accustomed to waiting for anything.

Martial arts educators need to understand, not only why parents are bringing children to them for fixing, but, more importantly, how the kids got broken in the first place. Because, unfortunately, this "right-now" culture cuts two ways. *Just as adult Americans are always looking for a quick solution to every problem, the constant social and psychological reinforcing of this same expectation of instant gratification causes their kids to lose confidence, self-esteem and patience.*

Think about these statistics: Eighty percent of children entering first grade have a positive attitude and high self-esteem, yet eighty percent of children entering third grade suffer from low self-esteem. Surprising, yes? And the reason isn't because they are two years older but rather due to having daily endured two years of negative input and bad influences while interacting with other children, parents, and teachers.

I am sure that a second grader who just struck-out playing baseball wouldn't be supported by his teammates with character-building comments like, "That was some great effort and concentration, Johnny! Keep up and persevere, and soon you will be hitting home runs!"

Instead, as mentioned in Chapter One, he or she is bombarded with comments, eighty percent of which are negative in nature. This constant negativity creates a belief system that soon begins to control the child's self-image, thinking and actions. *Understanding how this happens is the most important thing for any instructor dedicated to making positive life changes.* Our challenge is no different from the one facing an engineer who is designing a program to fix a defective automobile part. He, too, needs to understand what has gone wrong and caused the defect, before he can create a system to correct the situation.

Here we are, teaching martial arts which in themselves will not build the qualities parents expect to develop quickly. So, while we do see an opportunity to make these improvements happen, we are also faced with a major challenge. We have to do it *fast* because if we don't, not only will the parents become disappointed, but our students are going to quit, and then, of course, the opportunity is lost.

And there's another problem, too. Not only do we need to do it fast, we also must understand that our students are going to be constantly faced with their own challenges when they are not in class. In fact, out of the 112 waking hours during the week, we have only one-and-a-half hours to work our magic.

Now comes the most important mental shift instructors need in order to make this magic happen. Our thinking of our role as instructor must adjust. *We no longer teach martial arts, we now teach people.* Martial arts may be our subject, but the goals of the lessons are to empower students with the values and beliefs, so that they not only succeed in our schools and make it to black belt but also become a black belt 24/7. Becoming a black belt means that the student has internalized the lessons and is now a walking, talking, person of the integrity, pride and respect that we associate with a true black belt. He or she uses everything they are learning in the dojo to walk taller, to feel a stronger sense of self-worth backed by beliefs and values which will support smart decision-making and positive choices in every aspect of their life.

Let's not kid ourselves. This is not an easy change to make for the majority of "old school" martial arts instructors who were brought up training in the military or taught to excel in tournaments or street fights. Yet, if you asked an instructor what he or she most wants to be noted for, would it be to produce a handful of tournament competitors, or would it be to change your community by positively effecting hundreds of families? Would it be for a shelf full of trophies, or for the ability to help turn a shy child into a confident, goal-setting young adult who will lead a more fulfilling life because he trained at your school? I am sure the answer must be a resounding, "*yes!*" to the opportunity to be a teacher who can change lives.

Okay, cool - now we've got a mission to be proud of, one that is driven by a passion to make changes. Not so cool, however, the fact is that we have our hands tied by tradition. The martial arts curriculum works against us. The patterns, the one-steps, and other more complicated forms of our subject matter are likely to create a stumbling block simply because many talented adult athletes forget about the limitations of an average six-to-twelve year old who comes walking in our doors. So, if we are going to make the changes fast, it's not only *how* we are teaching, as mentioned in Chapter Two, but also *what* we are teaching.

Teaching a traditional art to most kids is no different than teaching algebra to a first grader. The majority just aren't going to get it. I am not saying a good teacher couldn't teach a small group of kids a traditional art. What I am saying is that it's much more difficult to impact hundreds of students at once and develop good life skills in them over a short period of time. So we need to teach simple arithmetic before going on to calculus.

All of this seems totally reasonable. Yet, just like their students do, instructors hold firm beliefs that things must be done in a certain way because that's the way they learned it. What makes matters worse is also fear of what their peers might be thinking. What if others perceive the changes you are making in terms of setting up "a belt factory" or "watering down" the arts? We can put aside these worries. Going back to the beginning of this book, I have talked about creating the "Universal System" for children, and how I was influenced by people like Tony Robbins and other motivators. They taught me the missing "E".

Great martial arts instructors know the secret is *"E-Cubed": Education, Entertainment and Empowerment*; and we have talked about two of these "E's" in detail. *Education* means teaching our students the life skills and values necessary to succeed in their training, so they can fully become *Empowered* in all aspects of their lives. The missing third "E" is *Entertainment*. If our classes are not Entertaining, then you will never be able to deliver the Education to Empower.

In Chapter Three, we talked about classroom management. The key to classroom management is that there are certain elements we can insert into the structure of every class to boost its entertainment value. Please, understand my meaning of "entertainment". Am I suggesting we become clowns or comedians? Absolutely not. However, I am suggesting we look at the structure of a great movie, play or TV show and understand what makes it so entertaining. We can then plug into our classes certain timetables of pacing and presentation, so that even our junior instructors can teach in a way that keeps students on "the edge of their seats" for the entire class.

Popular entertainment must immediately capture your attention. How often have you seen a terrific movie where the mystery is unfolded before the show begins? You only need to watch the beginning of the TV show "CSI" or "Law & Order" to understand how this works. More often than not, the body is found or the exciting scene unfolds even before the show starts. Within the first three to five minutes of "CSI", you are already anticipating and excited about watching the next 55 minutes; and then, all of a sudden, the credits come up and the soundtrack music by "*The Who*" begins. *That's entertainment!*

Well, how does this differ from what we are doing in our classes during the class management discussed in Chapter Three? There is no difference. Our dramatic "teasers" and "hooks" are a line-up with clapping, the running, a thundering student creed, a dynamic warm-up, creative and exciting drills for skills – these are all designed for class management. Movements and training to get your students up to a "level 10" must all happen even before you pre-frame what you are going to do in class today, which is to say, even before you reveal "the name of today's show".

We then go into the different scenes or chapters of the class, breaking down the class, like an episode of a show, into individual segments that are designed to educate in a very entertaining fashion. Each segment is an exiting aspect of martial arts training done in short blocks of time. We train in forms, self-protection, kicks – whatever your curriculum requires – using from ten to fifteen segments. That's enough time to make sure the students are getting better each day, yet short enough to keep the interest, focus and energy at a peak level.

My goal right now is not to re-teach the importance of class management but rather to demonstrate how Chapter Three is a key ingredient in "E-Cubed" – or the entertainment values built into class management.

Yet, even during the very best movie or TV show, there are always a couple of people who get up and walk out or start a little channel surfing. Although the majority of people who pick up my book are probably black belts with great determination, perseverance and tenacity, there was probably a time or two (and, more likely, three or more) when you have started something only to become distracted and quit. I know it's happened to me more than once.

There was that time when I was only two lessons from getting my private pilots license. To graduate, I needed to finish up by flying three cross-country trips solo. I don't care who you are – soloing in an airplane for the first time is scary. On my first run, I went from Plainville, Connecticut to Groton, to Newport, Rhode Island and then back home. I made the trip okay; however, I had a very rough landing in Newport. This was after about a year of lessons. The experience really rattled me, but, if I had an instructor who had kept after me, I probably would have gotten back on track.

I also started golf lessons at one time. I enrolled for twelve sessions but only took two. I missed my third, and you know how that is. You are a little embarrassed about going back, even though you want to. Also, after a week or two, the excitement and goals take a backseat to something else. Turns out, I never heard from the instructor again until about a year later when we met at a local restaurant. He came over and said hello, yet never even offered to continue the lessons.

Throughout my career, I can say I have saved many, many martial arts students from giving up and quitting. I've even been accused of caring more about my students' training than they did. Having this type of passion is vital if you are going to create a school of black belts and a portfolio of success stories. Remember the importance of calling and writing students who have gone missing in action. Always take the time for office mini-chats about changing goals. Recognize when a student's attendance starts slipping, and how good all our students feel when they receive that "good job" note or "awesome" card.

We started off talking about crossword puzzles. As the pieces come together for you, I hope you see the importance that compassion has in being a great instructor. More importantly, I hope you see how a thorough understanding of human nature is even more crucial. As our culture changes, so must our approach to teaching and instructing change.

Martial arts are a way of life. I don't know a black belt anywhere who would give up the education and experience martial arts have given them. Why, then, as martial arts instructors, would we want anything less for our students? When you look back at lessons and teachers you have had in the past, I am sure you can list a few great ones and a bunch of duds. Wouldn't it have been better if these grammar school, or horseback-riding, or teachers of other sports had possessed the passion and knowledge to educate you, entertain you, and empower you, all at the same time?

Now that you know there is a difference in teaching a subject and teaching people, you have no choice but to make sure your students will one day look back at their training with your and think, "Wow, was I ever lucky to have studied at that martial arts academy!" Or, "I was indeed fortunate to have an instructor who understood me and what I needed." Or, "I wouldn't give up that experience for a million dollars because martial arts made me a better and stronger person, and I credit earning a black belt with sparking my lifelong desire to help others."

Now, my friends, *that's* powerful!

CHAPTER NINE

BECOME REMARKABLE

I FEEL VERY CONFIDENT that the information we've shared so far can greatly increase your ability to make rapid changes in the students whom you serve. By applying the concept of "building black belts from the inside out," you should see students' life skills advance in a matter of months.

You will also notice that this added self-esteem and sense of pride and accomplishment will transform their physical abilities at warp speed, because they are not going to settle for a mediocre performance any longer. Instead, look forward to teaching students who want to be challenged and who feel a sense of urgency about raising their level to meet your expectations.

Yes, your students will change quickly, but you also need to get ready for a change that is going to happen to you. *You will inevitably want to have more students.* You are going to find teaching is easier, more fun and more rewarding. So you just aren't going to be satisfied anymore until you are making a large impact on the community you serve. Not by my rule, not because I say so, but because it's human nature to want to create an impact and to leave behind a proud legacy.

True story, to make my point... It's not only martial arts schools for whom this dynamic works so well.

For example, I am writing this chapter from Seville, Spain, at Epona Equestrian Center, which is a school for advanced equestrian riders and Andalusia horse enthusiasts. My wife and I are on a long-planned birthday trip in the company of Diego and Mary Beth Perez. Diego and Mary Beth own "*Better Families Through Tae Kwon Do*", in Miami, Florida, one of the largest single-body schools in the United States. It's great bouncing ideas off them and getting their feedback for this book. After all, they serve about nine-hundred students and two-hundred plus black belts, not counting the thousands of students in their "martial-arts-based" charter schools.

We are all staying at a hacienda with several other people from around the world. Now, I myself am not a rider, but everyone else is, so while they are out enjoying themselves, I get to sit in a beautiful courtyard and do some writing.

Overall, this entire experience is truly remarkable for everyone attending. During the mornings, they do a three-hour trail ride. Yesterday, it was through the fields and mountains, and today, it's on the beach. Every afternoon, they take another lesson with different instructors, according to their level of experience. On the "off" time and after dinner, they discuss nothing but the day's events. It's this constant talk about riding, learning and what they experienced that tells me it's truly remarkable here. I can assure you, everyone involved will continue to feel enthusiastic about their experience for a long, long, time to come.

So the family from China, the man from France, Pat from Scotland and the mother and daughter from

Spain are going to be walking, talking, advertisements for *Epona* in Seville. The old adage "The best advertising is word of mouth", is one-hundred-percent true. There is nothing like having a third person expounding on the benefits of your business to bring in a steady stream of qualified referrals. The key is to make your school REMARKABLE.

They say that someone who is happy with your service will tell one or two people. They also say that an unhappy customer will tell ten others of their negative experience. The goal in transforming your school into a REMARKABLE school is to turn that ratio around, so that each of your students is telling at least ten other people of their great experience of taking martial arts with you. I know many school owners around the country who are teaching literally several hundred students as a result of marketing the REMARKABLE way - by word of mouth.

Your first key ingredient for a REMARKABLE school is the physical look of your academy. I have had several very successful schools over three decades and many have taken on totally different appearances. My goal was always to create a unique atmosphere that was designed around my ideal student. *An ideal student is the profile of the main section of students you are marketing for.* In the seventies, my goal was to teach mainly adults, and my school had that grown-up feel, including weight training equipment, holes in the walls and a hardcore look and feel. However, in the early eighties, my student profile turned towards teaching children, and so the school was modified. It became very parent-friendly, with a great viewing area, magazines for moms, free coffee, inviting chairs, bulletin boards to show-off their kid's pictures, and, overall, the school was kept spotless. In the "Miami Vice" era of the late eighties, the colors got changed to pastels, and forty feet of neon lights were installed. My Coral Springs, Florida, school became the ultimate "cool" place to be in town. My competition was stuck in the white-wall-and-blue-carpet look; whereas, my school appeared to have been transplanted from South Beach.

Today, my school's interior is totally "urban", with brick walls, a diamond plate stainless-steel-and-cement octagon counter, nicely matted floors, high-top tables, wireless internet, fifty-inch flat screen TVs, a "killer sound system", surrounded by UFC fencing and a custom painted graffiti wall displaying our logo. Not your typical look for suburban Arizona, but definitely the hottest-looking facility within a hundred miles!

Not only am I trying to create a school that is fun and comfortable, including the latest training equipment, but one that students and parents will tell their friends about. This same school was only a basic studio when I bought it. I knew it had become REMARKABLE after the renovations because so many ex-students stopped by to take a look and told me, "I've been hearing that this school is beautiful – and it is!"

In the previous eight chapters, I have been detailing the importance of "E-cubed" classes; however, I can't stress enough the need for each and every class being your very best. *If you want students to remark about your school, then give them something to talk about.* I will get to special events later, but right now I want to discuss a couple of things you should be doing daily to make sure your students have a thing or two to tell people about.

Students should be bragging about their instructors. Your instructors must "walk the talk" and be outstanding role models of martial artists. Students should be telling their friends how fast you are, how well you can kick, what a great guy or gal you are, how friendly you are, and all about your accomplishments as a martial artist. Just a reminder - of course, you can tell them, but they must see it to believe it. A plaque on the wall or a picture of you standing beside a movie star – that's one thing. However, the way you present yourself every single day is what impresses your students. And, *when they aren't talking about you, they ought to be talking about themselves, because you make their experience so special.* It might be because of the recognition they are getting, a new stripe, being "Leader of the Day", receiving a "good job" note, making "Student of the Month" or a host of other things you can do to make that student's day.

Your parents should also find plenty to chat about. They should be so educated about your school's purpose and mission that they are ready to spring into referral action every time a co-worker or friend mentions any challenges with their own children. You can educate parents about your mission during mat chats to students, by teaching benefits in class, using life skill worksheets, through your newsletter, stripe testing, and graduation. They must understand your school gives an education as valuable as elementary or middle school.

In fact, it should be your goal that, on the parents' list of values, church may be first, family second, but then should come their child's education at your martial arts school. They need to believe you have a balanced approach to martial arts, and that you find teaching life skills just as important as the physical movements. When a co-worker mentions that he or she is having discipline challenges with their child, the first thing any parent of your students should do is to give them a guest pass while telling them exactly how your school can make a difference in the child's life. I can tell you, with one-hundred percent confidence, that I have gone to schools, taught the staff how to integrate life skills and benefit teaching and literally tripled their referrals in thirty days.

Parents must also see their kids develop physically. I often shrink down in my chair when I'm watching classes at some schools that don't make corrections. Or else, they accept substandard performances from their students. I mean, come on! What parent is going to lean over to the person next to them while watching class and say, "Check out the kid in the back doing everything backwards. *That's my boy!*" It's ridiculous, correct?

So give your parents bragging rights. Train their child to improve coordination, power and speed. Make sure that when your student scores that next home run in Little League that all the other parents understand it's the skills the child has learned in martial arts that have made the huge difference in him on the ball field. Not only has his reaction time improved, but, because he is stronger physically, and more confident, it's no wonder he is excelling at other things, as well. To make this clear, you need to constantly educate the parents on what to look for outside of the martial arts school, that is a result of what the child is learning inside the school.

What will your students and parents say next time someone asks them, "So what did you do this weekend?" It happens every Monday to probably eighty-five percent of the folks involved with your school. Are they going to mention the ball game they watched, the movie they saw, or will they remark about an event at your school?

"This weekend was amazing. You know, my daughter takes martial arts at ABC Martial Arts, and they held graduation on Friday night. I am not sure how this school does it, but they never cease to amaze me. Samantha was awarded her blue belt. The ceremony was great. I think the best part was when her dad and I got to actually tie the new belt around her. We are not usually that emotional, but the instructor had all the students tell their parents why they are so proud of them as parents, and my eyes just watered up."

"And, wow! The school went above and beyond and held the graduation at the high school. You know, it's the largest martial arts school in town by far because it's so good. The instructor put on an amazing show, I think she broke at least twelve boards, and after it was all over, they treated all the students and parents to a free Chinese buffet. I think that martial arts is one of the best things we've done for Samantha. It started out just as a way for her to learn self-defense, but now she is doing forms, her confidence has improved, and it's showing up in better school grades. And by the way, the school is allowing us to give free VIP memberships to friends. Do you think your son, David, would like to go?"

The fact is people will talk about you like that once you give them a reason to talk like that. Or, okay, how about this? "My husband and I had the best Friday night out in a long time. It was funny because we never go on date nights any more, but my son Brandon's martial arts school held a Parents Night Out, party. He wanted to go, so we decided to take advantage of the opportunity and had a great dinner and went to a movie. That martial arts school is incredible! They are always doing something for the kids or the parents."

I can't say this often enough. Remember, *people will talk if you give them something to talk about.* You should constantly bring in guest instructors for seminars, conduct special parties, picnics, sleepovers and events, not only to make your school the "social place to be", but, more importantly, to give students and parents something to talk about. "I mean, the school is just remarkable!"

Once you have your parents and students remarking about your school, it's time to take things to a new level. *You must become a public relations master.* This is where you take advantage of the media to get people talking about your school. So, instead of just getting one-on-one referrals, your school will be marketed to thousands of people in a single day. This can be done on several levels.

First, you need to understand that, if something is happening at your school which is interesting to a large portion of your community, the newspapers, TV and radio will be interested, too. Many schools send out news releases when a student wins a local tournament. This is, of course, interesting to your school and to the student's family but does not necessarily carry the news-value clout to gain wide-spread media coverage.

However, if you have helped a family whose son or daughter has overcome a learning disability, then you have elevated yourself into an expert in the field and can offer a possible solution to other families with similar problems. If your school is active in community events, or your demo team donated their time to perform at the Assisted Living Home, you have a "human interest story" of value. On an even larger scale, if your school sponsors a tournament or break-a-thon to support a national charity, and hundreds of students and families are there supporting the event, you can almost be sure that your local TV station will air a segment.

It all comes down to involvement in the community and your commitment to helping others. But, don't think I will do a charity event just so I can get on TV. Instead, as part of your overall curriculum, plan on how your school can get involved in teaching your students the importance of giving back and of helping others. Once you are on the right unselfish mission, people will talk and talk, and your school becomes more and more REMARKABLE.

"You can have everything in life you want, if you will just help enough other people get what they want."

– Zig Ziglar

A word of caution – Once you get your school to this level, your competition is also going to talk about you. However, never forget, when someone talks behind your back, it only means you are two steps ahead of them!

CHAPTER TEN

KEEPING YOUR BLACK BELTS YOUR BLACK BELTS

YOUR BLACK BELTS

THROUGHOUT THIS BOOK we have been stressing the importance of becoming a great teacher and creating a positive, empowering experience for our students from day one. We then touched upon the importance of attracting new students because I know that once you have mastered bringing out the best in students and you find your position more enjoyable and teaching easier, you just won't be happy until you are making a significant impact on your community. The only thing more rewarding than helping and positively changing the lives of one-hundred-fifty families is impacting three-hundred families. I can also tell you that when you impact one-thousand families in your community, *you have transformed yourself from the local "karate guy" to a leader and expert in your community and nothing will make you more fulfilled and happy.*

You have most likely heard the analogy that building a school is like filling a bucket with water. School owners are always adding water or new students into the bucket; however, those darn holes in the bottom of the bucket make it seem impossible to ever fill the bucket. What you have learned in "*The Silva Solution*" so far will close most of those holes *if properly applied.* I want to make this clear because knowledge isn't necessarily power and is not guaranteed to make a difference. Applying your knowledge and having a mindset of continuous improvement will get your to where you want to be and can be life-changing.

We now face a new challenge that very few school owners ever face. That challenge is *not losing students from the bottom of the bucket, but rather having your bucket overflow.*

You see, a great school with solid instruction and student service will inevitably promote many black belts, which is just what we want. Since many schools rarely see fifty to two-hundred active black belts, they haven't experienced the challenge this presents. For as loyal as someone becomes on their way to black belt, it is not uncommon for someone to tune into W.I.F.M (What's In it For Me) if they become idle. They then become your ex-student or even worse... your competition.

As I mentioned in the last chapter, I was in Spain this spring and had an incredible opportunity to travel from Seville to Madrid by train with Diego and Mary Beth Perez, from Miami. They are two of the martial arts industry business leaders. As I mentioned, their school *Better Families through Tae Kwon Do* has about nine-hundred members, but even more impressive is that they have two-hundred active black belts with two of those holding the rank of fourth degree. During this undisturbed two hours I told them about my idea for this chapter and asked it they wouldn't mind brain-storming the topic, "What does it take to retain Black Belts?" It was my goal to make a list of eight points, but, to my delight and the readers' benefit, we discovered fifteen very important topics.

Here they are – not in any special order. Of course, if I had my way they would all be number one!

1. KEEP YOUR BLACK BELTS HUMBLE.

From day-one at most schools, earning a black belt is the ongoing goal of students. We talk about "black belt excellence" throughout the lessons as a way of motivating students to be their best or at least to try their best. Most schools use the motto, "THIS IS A BLACK BELT SCHOOL" as a way of conveying the importance of commitment and perseverance.

There is so much emphasis on this achievement, it's no wonder that once students reaches the rank of black belt, their egos tend to get a little inflated. In fact, many instructors and school owners are downright afraid students will quit right away because the student feels that they are "done", that they've made it. I've even seen some schools adopt a policy that students must sign another contract before they test or else the school will hold their diploma for a year as a way of making sure the student sticks around.

What often makes it worse is that same tired old speech so many instructors give during black belt tests. The message is that, "a black belt is when you really start to learn, and not a final goal." Wow! Talk about taking the wind out of a students sail. They are sitting there all excited, feeling a sense of accomplishment and all of a sudden they learn that they are just ready to learn! "Hey, I thought this was supposed to be a big deal. What a waste of time! I'm out of here."

Black Belt is a great goal and students should set it. Instructors should also use it as a motivating tool. However, students need to understand there is life after the goal is reached. They should realize they have reached a high level of proficiency *but not the final level.*

The concept of "kaizen", or constant and never-ending improvement, is extremely important. *Wearing a black belt should mean that you have become a black belt, not been given a black belt.* Becoming a black belt means that you have internalized patience, humility, contribution, etc. As an instructor to black belts, we must keep them humble by showing them there is still more to learn and, at the same time, keep perfecting their old material and basics. We can't allow them to feel they have mastered everything. We do this by refining our teaching, so they learn the details and continue to further understand concepts and principles of material they already think they have down pat.

1. BLACK BELTS NEED ADDITIONAL CURRICULUM

When I first became a black belt in 1973, I had asked my instructor what comes next. He laid out the plan like this... For each additional rank, there was a timeframe corresponding to the rank. He said that second degree required two years of training. After that, third degree was three years of training, fourth was four years, etc.

Okay, that's fair. Even at age twenty-three, I could understand the concept and appreciate the time and dedication. I was also excited by thinking, "This is amazing! Can you imagine how much I will be learning?" (only to find out later it was one new form per degree.) One of the needs people have is for growth and advancement. In order to keep your black belts actively training, you must have a well-structured curriculum.

People love to learn something new. This may mean that, as the master instructor, you have to learn more to have more to pass on. It might mean structuring your present program so that you don't teach everything before black belt and have nothing left to offer after black belt. When I had my school in Connecticut, I opted to keep learning, which meant traveling weekly to Baltimore to continue my training with a high-ranking instructor. The point here is to realize that, if you really intend to offer long-term instruction and to keep your black belts active and loyal, you must have a long-term curriculum and not one that only lasts the first thirty-six months.

2. DON'T TAKE YOUR BLACK BELTS FOR GRANTED

Are you thinking this? "Our black belts have been around for years. Most have been "A" students for as long as they have been highly supportive of the school, attended events, volunteered to help out here and there – I mean, these people are lifers." *This attitude can be very destructive.*

Yes, they have been here for a long time, but this doesn't mean they have become blindly loyal and would never think of quitting. In fact, they are probably thinking just the opposite of you. You are thinking about how this person has been here for five years, and you have bent over backwards for him or her during all that time. On the contrary, now that they are black belts, they need to understand that it's their obligation to help the school.

"Hey," you might suppose, "I have all these new students, so my veterans can just work on their old stuff or teach a few beginners for me." On the other hand, the veterans might be thinking, "I've been loyal to this school. I've paid my tuition for years and continue to pay. However, the school seems to being taking me for granted. Aren't black belts supposed to be special? Shouldn't I be the one getting the attention? Heck, I've paid him almost $10,000 and volunteered tons of times. Fair is fair, so what has this school done for me lately?"

Now I am not going to defend either position. I am just going to share a truth. No matter how thin you slice a piece of bread, there are always two sides. Whatever your customers perceive to be the truth, is the truth to them. Keep in mind the one thing that has never changed since the student was a white belt. *We don't teach martial arts, we teach people.* Martial arts are simply the subject matter. Black belts are people with the same needs as white belts, so be sure to make them feel special.

3. RENEW GOALS AND SET TESTING DEADLINES.

Students are used to requirements, testing goals and stripe testing on their journey to black belt. It is this system that is so successful at keeping students on track and active in their training. Once a student becomes a black belt, he or she needs to continue with goal-setting, and having deadlines to meet. Resetting goals will keep the students interest high. Having a deadline to meet creates a sense of urgency and reason to train consistently.

4. DEFEND YOUR BLACK BELT

We know the need to continuously review and perfect the basics and curriculum that got us to black belt, for black belt isn't the destination, but merely a mile-marker on our journey.

Mary Beth Perez was telling me a story about meeting a high-ranking instructor at a tournament. She had mentioned to him that she was looking forward to learning this new form and asked the instructor if one of his students would demonstrate it for her. The master instructor said, "Sure, we would be glad to," and asked one of his black belts to perform it. The black belt seemed to forget it about halfway through. The next black belt student also didn't remember the form, nor did the third. Mary Beth said she then wondered, "Are you still a black belt if you've forgotten your requirements that got you there?"

The Perez's adopted a policy of spontaneous black belt classes where students remove their belts and put them at the front of the room. The students must then "Defend Their Black Belts" by passing an intensive review. This simple system demonstrates to the students the importance of keeping up on former training as well as always looking great and performing sharply. It's also a worthy challenge that gives the students a chance for some healthy competition.

5. SPECIALIZED TRAINING

In order to keep interest high, improve performance and make them feel special, your black belts should have specialized training in addition to their regular curriculum. These could be special curriculum classes you teach, seminars with guest instructors, or traveling and training with a special instructor.

What a great feeling it is for high ranking students to be offered training that is only for their level! It not only feels special but also improves the bond among your high-level students, and they then appreciate you and your school more. They understand you have a special interest in their progress and continued education.

I often hear about a black belt cross-training in another system or style, to learn more. This then creates a tension between the student and instructor. The instructor feels the student is disloyal. The solution is simple. If you realize this is going to happen, instead of letting your top students train somewhere else, you offer the training at your own school though seminars and guest instructors.

6. RECOGNITION FOR ADVANCEMENT

We have already discussed the need for resetting goals, setting deadlines and learning new curriculum. This is necessary so the students, no matter what rank, keeping making progress. However, in addition to progress, the student must be recognized. In the lower ranks it's easy, what with the awarding of a new color belt or stripe. However, once a student reaches black belt, you need to get creative about finding fresh ways to show advancement.

A friend of mine in Arizona, Master Fred DePalma, has a unique way of doing this through what he calls "black belt grades". These are not degrees but grades in between the degrees. The student is recognized for achievement by having their belt embroidered with their name in different colors. So as to not complicate this too much, the method is, black belts with their name embroidered in yellow have been black belts longer and have learned more than a black belt with their name embroidered in white. Mr. DePalma understood the need for not only setting goals but devised a way to recognize advancement for his black belts.

7. BLACK BELT UNIFORMS AND CERTIFICATES

Simple enough – just give your black belts a special "look" and image that is only for them. When I fly Delta, I can easily spot the difference between the captain of the aircraft and a flight attendant. Your black belts should have their own look and identity and should be instantly recognized for their achievement.

Speaking of uniforms for black belts, it's a great touch when you sell a uniform to a black belt, to make sure all the school emblems and patches are already sewn on, and it's embroidered with his or her name. This is just one of those added services that elevate the status of being a black belt.

We do the same thing if we are presenting a diploma or certificate to a black belt. The diploma is always in a very nice frame under glass and ready to hang. Everything is done to show special recognition.

8. SPECIAL EVENTS

We talked earlier about specialized training, but in addition to curriculum training, are "black belt only" special events. The purpose is to strengthen the social element of your school. Students who have special ties to the group are less likely to quit because it's not just stopping an activity, it is more like losing your friends and family. Some special events should be totally social, like a holiday dinner or cookout. Other events may be martial arts related, such as a twenty-four hour boot camp.

Again, the event itself is important, but the main thing is to *realize the powerful impact social activities have on retention.* The only thing more powerful is to have an event exclusively for only the top students or black belts.

9. GET INVOLVED AT THE FAMILY LEVEL

We have a very strict rule in our school that instructors do not socialize with students. We do everything possible to make sure the student–teacher relationship is totally professional and to insure that nothing compromises this relationship. Students and teachers become friends during the course of training, and students will want to invite you to social events; however, I feel it's important that we keep our private life separate from our professional ones.

The only time this changes is at the black belt level. Your black belts become extended family. I am not suggesting we become buddies and go out for a beer after class, but I am suggesting you invite your black belts to holiday parties, and you might possibly reciprocate by attending their birthday parties, weddings and important social events. It means a lot to your students at the black belt level to have you around and be able to introduce their instructor to friends and family members. If you have done you job well, they will view you as someone who helped form their lives and will be proud of this association.

10. ELEVATED LEVEL OF RESPECT AND PROTOCOL

Black belts have earned the respect and seniority to be addressed as Mr., Ms., or Mrs. This applies to all students and staff members. Up to this point, students may call each other by their first names; however, it's another level of respect when one puts on their black belt. Not only are they addressed by their surnames but should also be given respect by lower ranks prior to and at the end of class.

This added protocol and respect adds to the overall experience of being a black belt student. Always remember how our goal is never to lose students at this level. Learning new material is important, yes, but it is the entire experience you create at your academy which makes being part of your organization one that people are attracted to and do not want to leave.

11. YEARLY SPEECH AND ESSAY

One of their projects and/or responsibilities is for black belts to address the student body at testing or graduations. Each year, one task is to express, both on paper and in a presentation to other students, the impact your school and martial arts have made on them in the past year.

It's one thing for you to constantly impress on your black belts the effect martial arts training has. It's totally different and more effective when they are expressing to lower ranks what the school and program has done for them in the past twelve months. Don't forget, it's your job to make sure your upper-belts can answer the question, "What has the school done for me lately?" By doing this exercise, they are identifying what you have done and expressing their gratitude publicly. They are helping to maintain the student body while discovering for themselves the power of a martial arts lifestyle.

12. MISSING IN ACTION

It's inevitable, no matter how much we enjoy something, that we, at times, get off-track. With work, families, and everything else that happens in our lives, students, even our top students, will miss class, occasionally. When this happens to your black belts, it should be the responsibility of the master instructor to call and make sure everything is all right.

This, again, is different that the regular systems of the school where it's probably your front counterperson who would do such a chore. It's your goal to make sure your black belts know that you care more about their training than maybe even they do. Not only that you care about their training, but you are concerned about them on a personal level, as well.

13. LEADERSHIP POSITION

Your black belts need to have leadership responsibilities. These responsibilities are designed so that other under-belt students are relying on them for guidance. It may be easy to let yourself drop out, however, when someone else is looking up to you for leadership, that becomes a new and more important level of commitment.

These duties include participating on the board of exams for future testing and mentoring students preparing for the black belt exam. And your current black belts should always have a student they mentor by motivating them, providing guidance and assistance in training. It's their goal to make sure their sponsor student passes the black belt exam with flying colors. Once black belts are part of something much bigger than themselves, they see their position at the school change and will look forward to participating each week.

14. BLACK BELT BOARD OF HONOR

The black belt board of honor is simply your school's or system's family tree. A nice oak board with the school's black belts and levels of rank professionally engraved on a brass plaque makes a huge statement when displayed at the school. Once your name is there, it's forever. Your name on the Board of Honor or family tree is a statement that you are part of the system that will be passed down from instructor to student for a long, long, time to come.

I hope you felt the sense of pride, accomplishment, respect and honor that we continuously show our upper-belts. This experience won't be duplicated in anything else they do... with the possible exception of owning a Harley Davidson. Seriously, think about this. Harley Davidson has created a culture for owners of Harleys that only they can understand. It's not just the bike, the clothes, the tattoos or the leathers. It's being part of the culture that keeps owners totally loyal to the brand. Even when Harleys were known for breaking-down and oil leaks, owners still bought a Harley over anything else.

These guidelines will help you create the same, "Harley Davidson-strong" culture and loyalty with your school.

CHAPTER ELEVEN

THE LAST CHAPTER OF THIS BOOK — HOWEVER, THE STORY IS NOT OVER...

AS A TEACHER, I have an incredible opportunity because I am not limited only to the impression I make on the students lining up in my class. I also make an impact on the hundreds of thousands of students who are training at schools I consult with, internationally. Now, with the release of this book, I hope you, too, and others reading and implementing these ideas, will all go on to make martial arts training a life-changing experience for those you have an influence on.

While getting ready to write this last chapter, the schools that I consult for were preparing for the monthly stripe or TIP testing at their individual academies. I understand the impact, both positive and negative that this monthly experience has on our students, and so, I sent the following short e-mail out to all the instructors.

Good Morning

Today and tomorrow are super-exciting days for your school. It's stripe testing, and your opportunity to make your students feel great, to set them up for success and give them an opportunity to celebrate a victory.

I mention this because I was shocked by a call I had yesterday. It went something like this: "Man, I have a brother and sister in my classes that I could do without. I can't wait to fail them on stripe test. Hopefully, then they will quit."

I couldn't believe what I was hearing! This is an instructor who has the amazing opportunity to change a family's life – *and he is going to make these kids feel even more rejected?!*

Take some time before you hit the floor today and reflect on what it means to a student when they reach a milestone. Then, plan what you can do to make sure your students remember today as a magic moment. I have included a sample after-stripe test speech for you.

First, however, let's talk briefly about Incentive Program (TIP) testing. It's important you understand that each month every student in your school should be tested for a stripe on their belt. This is one of the keys to teaching students goal-setting as well as your chance to give each student a well-deserved pat on the back.

Okay, on with the speech! Let's imagine that we have just finished stripe testing. My "Ya Gotta Be Here" speech would go something like this:

"I just want to congratulate everyone on a job well done. That stripe on your belt is more than just a piece of electrical tape. It is a sign that you have made progress towards your next goal. It signifies that you have attended class, did hundreds of kicks and hundreds of punches and improved. You could have sat around the house like many kids, but you did something positive. You applied yourself to a worthwhile goal that will help every aspect of your life. You shouldn't walk in the door tonight at home. No. When you get home, you should glide on air – that's how proud you should be of yourself."

"When we succeed at a goal, we should do two things. First, celebrate! So, give yourself a big hand and a pat on the back. Second, we need to reset a new goal. Now, next week you "gotta be here". That is the week we will learn the first part of the material for your next stripe. So, where do you have to be next week? That's right! Here for two classes."

I then received this e-mail from a client and good friend of mine, Paul McCoy from Massachusetts: "If we did not have students who needed our help, we would be unemployed. Famous quote: 'Oh, hear this,' he said to them. If they were not sick, what need would they have of a doctor?"

"Stripe testing is the proof that we are valid, and a test of both the student's ability as a martial artist – and, by extension, everything else – and our test as an instructor.

Some fly over the bar, some jump, some fall, some we need to encourage, some to threaten and, more than most, some we need to throw over the bar. It is the act of going over and knowing that you did eventually do it that builds success."

That afternoon, I was watching the stripe testing evaluation at my school in Mesa, Arizona. It was the beginning kids' class, and I was just sitting in the back of the room taking everything in. I noticed Jason, a new student in class, who took a position in the back corner of the room. The class did the warm-up and some drills for skills, and then the instructor asked them to line up again in front of the wave master bags for some drills on their kicks. Again, our new student found his way to the back of the room and the far wave master, which was just in front of me. I immediately sensed his lack of self-confidence and recognized this as a golden opportunity to start to change that.

At my school, I use hand signals to communicate with the instructors on the floor. I was able to get Master Fiori's attention, pointed to the student in the back and then to my eyes and heart. Mr. Fiori instantly got the message to watch Jason and give him some extra attention. Being an instructor with a "critical eye," he also noticed a lack of confidence in Jason and took immediate action.

"Jason," he said, "I've got to tell you that you have to be the bravest kid in class today. Not only are you trying very hard, you have also lined up in the back in front of Grandmaster Silva for each drill. That takes an incredible amount of courage and confidence. I just had to tell you how impressed I am with you."

Jason's reaction was priceless; his body posture changed, and he was smiling from ear to ear. Mr. Fiori didn't stop there. He saw the difference in Jason now and wanted to anchor this magic moment one more time. A few minutes later, he had the class sit down and "spot-lighted" Jason in front of the class, demonstrating his strong stance and warrior face.

In the first part of this book, I mentioned Carl, the student who had gone bald at age six and began training at my school in Connecticut. I wrote before how, if Carl was ever to make it to black belt, he would need the "Miagi" treatment – Mr. Miagi being the instructor in the movie, "The Karate Kid" who built Daniel into a confident young man. I sat there and thought, "Here I am, twenty-five years later, and another opportunity has crossed my path to make a huge difference in someone's life through martial arts. What an amazing career I have chosen."

After class, I stepped outside to say congratulations to students as they left the school. All of a sudden, Jason and his sister came up to me. I almost got out congratulations when his sister began talking.

"Master Silva, guess who is older? I'll tell you. I am one minute older than my brother. Not only that, I am smarter too. I do gymnastics and don't even take karate, and I can still kick higher than my brother...." And on, and on she went.

My first thought was to have her put some sparring gear on, but she was only about eight years old. So, instead, "Very good," I said, "Did you see how good Jason did on his stripe test?"

"Yeah, he did good," she responded.

"Well, can you do me a big favor?" I asked. "I know you can do it because, as you say, you are very smart.

Would you please tell Jason how happy you are for him for doing so well?"

She did, too. It may have not been the most sincere congratulations, but I could tell it made Jason happy.

The entire staff is now aware that Jason is being bullied 24/7 by his sister, and we have made it our project to help him by building this black belt from the inside out using all the tools I mention in this book.

Do you have a student or students who could use the same treatment? As Paul McCoy wrote in response to my stripe testing e-mail, "Some fly over the bar, some jump, some fall, some we need to encourage over, some to threaten and more than most, some we need to throw over the bar. It is the act of going over and knowing that you did eventually do it that builds success."

Do what it takes to make those positive experiences and magical moments for your students. There is a lot of information presented in this book. Some may have been reminders of concepts you have heard before, and some was new, enlightening and, hopefully, inspiring. I trust I also conveyed the great opportunity you have, as well as the responsibility. You are now faced with the decision of when and how you are going to make changes.

It is my suggestion that you think of the following: "Anything worth doing, is worth doing poorly until you perfect it." In other words, too often people put off and wait until they have mastered something to put it to use. However, when it comes to something that could be life-changing or worth doing, you shouldn't wait because all too often it will fall to the wayside. If it's that important, get started today and begin to master and perfect the concepts as you go.

I was asked to speak at a business meeting many years ago. At that time, I was comfortable teaching martial arts but very nervous doing this presentation in front of non-martial arts businessmen. Before I spoke, while pacing in the hallway, a man walked by wearing a Tony Robbins t-shirt. On the back, it read, "If you can't, you must. If you must, you will". I thought, "I am believing right now I can't do this presentation. I don't like that feeling, so 'I must do it'."

Not only did I do it, I put everything I had into making it a good presentation. Now, maybe it wasn't my best; over the years I have gotten totally comfortable and much better. But, if I had waited to get good before I even tried, I would have made a huge mistake. So, my advice is to get out there today and begin to make changes. And, please, share your stories with me for my next book. Like I titled this chapter "Chapter 11 – The last chapter of this book – However, the story is not over..."

Oh, by the way, this was in my e-mail box today, and it relates to the e-mail I began this chapter with, since it also shows the results of taking action.

Hello Mr. Silva,

I just wanted to write a quick note to you. I really appreciated the email you sent recently, regarding uplifting students after their stripe test. I repeated it to my students today after their stripes were awarded and they were so happy. They left class with a "joyous buzz", and were high-fiving each other. Thanks for the HUGE tip.

– Wanda J White

I really enjoy hearing about the successes enjoyed by instructors who take my advice because it makes me feel that I have been right to sit down and write this book and let you all in on the *Silva Solution*. Good luck!

END